DANCING
WITH
YOUR HORSE

DANCING
WITH
YOUR HORSE

Mary E. Campbell
Foreword by Anne Gribbons

Half Halt Press
Middletown, Maryland

Dancing With Your Horse
© 1989 Mary E. Campbell

Published in the United States of America by
Half Halt Press, Inc.
6416 Burkittsville Road
Middletown, MD 21769

Jacket design by Clara Graves
Text designed and typeset by Rebecca Hocker

U.S.D.F. Freestyle Score Sheets reproduced by the kind
permission of the Unites States Dressage Federation, Inc.

A.H.S.A. Freestyle Score Sheets and excerpts from *Rule
Book* reproduced by the kind permission of the American
Horse Shows Association, Inc.

Library of Congress Cataloging-in-Publication Data

Campbell, Mary E.,   1924-
    Dancing with your horse / by Mary E. Campbell ; foreword by Anne
Gribbons.
        p.   cm.
    ISBN 0-939481-17-0 : $20.00
    1. Musical freestyle rides (Dressage)   I. Title.
SF309.6C35   1989
798.2'3--dc20   89-24490
                                                    CIP

Table of Contents

Acknowledgments 7

Foreword by Anne Gribbons 9

Thoughts about "Freestyle-Kür" in Dressage Riding
by Dr. Joseph Knipp 11

Chapter 1:
The Musical Freestyle 13

Chapter 2:
Basic Principles in Musical Freestyle 17
    The Horse's Gaits 17
    Rhythm 18
    Tempo.. 20

Chapter 3:
A Little Music Theory 23
    What is a Beat? 23
    Measures, Bar Lines and Double Bar Lines 26
    Note Values 27
    Time Signatures 29
    Phrases 31

Chapter 4
Getting Started 33
    How to Determine and Use Beats per Minute 33
    Timers 34
        Metronomes 34
        Kitchen Timers 35
        Stopwatches 35
    Counting Beats per Minute 36
        Trot 38
        Walk 39

Canter 39
A Note on Timing Passage and Piaffe 40
Timing Music 41

Chapter 5
Working with Music 43
Styles of Music 43
Folk Music 44
Latin Music 45
Ragtime 45
American Modern 46
Other Styles of Music 47
Suitability of Music to Horse and Rider 49
Music Sources 50
Listening to Music 51
The Music Library 52
The Practice Tape 54
Lungeing to Music 55

Chapter 6:
Creating Your Musical Freestyle Ride 57
Choreographing the Ride 60
Timing and Editing the Ride 64
Adding the Music 65
A Special Word About Entrance Music 66

Chapter 7:
Preparing the Cassette Tape 71
Cassette Tapes 71
Boom Box 72
Recording Instructions for Making a Cassette Tape ... 73
Preparing the Tape for the Choreographed Ride 76
Using a Recording Studio 78
Speed Changes 81
Some Final Tips 82

Appendix 1:
Official Score Sheets 83

Appendix 2:
Diagrams of Musical Freestyle Rides 99

Index 123

Acknowledgments

There are many people who have over the years contributed to the development of this book, both directly and indirectly. It would not be an overstatement to say that I have learned something from every rider and horse combination with whom I've worked preparing music for freestyle rides. There are a few people, though, whose contributions deserve special recognition.

Anne Gribbons, one of America's topmost dressage musical freestyle riders, shared her time to present the foreword to *Dancing With Your Horse*. Anne also deserves a commendation for her work with the junior/young riders of America.

In his *Thoughts about "Freestyle - Kür in Dressage Riding*, Dr. Josef Knipp, an FEI I judge from West Germany, clearly gives us an unparalleled understanding of what and how the harmony of the horse and rider should be for a musical freestyle.

Nancy Harris shared her choreography for the Fourth Level Freestyle ride found in Appendix 2. A versatile horsewoman, Nancy's awards and credits are numerous. In addition, she was the first presenter of a musical freestyle ride that beamed and started me scrambling to find a way to the new dance form.

Bent Jensen, who contributed the Intermediate and Grand Prix Freestyle rides in this book, generously shared hours of his time. A former Danish National Champion, and now a dressage trainer competing at top level shows, he has gained the respect of his peers. Bent excells through his progressive training and precise technical riding skills.

In addition, I especially want to thank my husband Bob, a musician who initiated the theory for *Dancing With Your Horse*, and who has spent countless hours working with music, many at ringside to make it work.

Foreword

My introduction to Mary Campbell is fairly recent, but it didn't take me long to realize that her enthusiasm for riding to music is no "Johnny come lately." It was hard to tell when I talked to her which aspect she preferred—the equestrian or the audio. . . . and perhaps that fact is the most appealing aspect of Mary Campbell's new book on musical freestyle. Because Mrs. Campbell is a rider as well as an educated musician, she flows effortlessly from one area to the other, dealing comfortably and capably with both subjects.

Whether you have ridden numerous freestyles or are a true beginner at it, this book will offer something of value. I found myself intrigued with the explanation of how to count the beats per minute at the different paces of the horse and the description of how to integrate the phases of the music into a smooth program. We learn how to choose, measure and organize the music to fit a particular horse and it is depressing to realize how far the inspiring tune you just heard on the radio is from becoming your horse's perfect freestyle beat.

Again and again Mrs. Campbell refers to the similarities between dancing and riding to music. Being an avid dancer myself I always felt the two activities to be closely related—although the horse lacks the ability to adapt to the music the way a human can. Instead, in Campbell-fashion, we tailor the notes to fit the horse until he looks like an equine Fred Astaire.

The way I have always put my program together is by selecting the music first and then fitting the choreography to the music. Mary Campbell takes the opposite approach: she encourages the rider to diagram the ride and *then* add the music, thus being able to match every step of the horse to the proper music. I admit I was skeptical—but it does work!

The book covers every aspect of creating a freestyle ride, and then some. Dealing with choreography Mrs. Campbell even includes some sample rides from each AHSA level. Not only the artistic aspect of constructing the music tape is dealt with, but also the technical end.

Throughout the book Mrs. Campbell manages to disguise the fact that this is actually a "how-to" manual by making personal comments and livens the text by cheering the reader on. The author loves both horses and music—she knows her subject and she'll make you want to invite your horse to dance!

Thoughts About "Freestyle-Kür" in Dressage Riding

by Dr. Josepf Knipp

I would like to say a few words about freestyle riding because it is new and still in a state of development and many people do not see clearly its purpose.

Handling and working with horses is not only a pastime or fitness-training but also for improving oneself, i.e. self-education. Classical Dressage in our sense is the development of inherent potentialities and natural abilities of a horse with the result of making the horse calm, supple and keen, thus achieving a perfect understanding and harmony with his rider.

Dressage is a visual art and both rule and tradition dictate that the horse be superbly turned out. Dressage is rooted in antiquity and even the riding of freestyle has a long tradition. Already in the 17th century there were so-called "horse-ballets" with music. Today, freestyle tests are very attractive and they are an enrichment for dressage riding. The aim is to make dressage more popular.

The required movements and exercises are not shown in the same sequence like in a corresponding test. Moreover, the rider has the opportunity of free composition of his program with the possibility to emphasize special merits and abilities of his horse in accordance with the music. Here, the rider has an outlet for creative energy. The composition of the program gives the rider an opportunity to show the degree of training of his horse and to develop a special feeling for music and creativity. But above all, the rules of "classical dressage" should be the basis and strictly observed. Freestyle-riding is of high value for the rider too because the music teaches him to develop a "feeling for rhythm."

The artistic expression of a harmonious presentation—where the choreography corresponds to the music—increases the quality, brillance and grace of a performance. The rider should show some risque in experimenting. The rhythm of the music should be the same as the rhythm of the horse's movement. Consequently the different gaits would require different types of music. But, if the gaits change too often, the music has to change often too and this causes a kind of disharmony in the whole picture and fluidity of the performance. Music should not be just background music—and it never should be "Pop against Art."

You can compare freestyle-riding with ice-skating. In both kinds of sport, music transcends to the movement. The difference is, of course, that here we have two living beings. This requires a different system of evaluation. The evaluation of a freestyle-test consists of one mark for technical execution and one for the artistic presentation. The technical score consists of the sum of the marks for the compulsory movements. The evaluation of the artistic presentation consists of the points for: harmony between rider and horse, the ease of the movements, the composition of the program, the choreography, i.e. new ideas, originality, symmetrical figures, using the whole arena, the degree of difficulty and, last but not least, the incorporation and interpretation of the music by the horse's movements is of great importance.

So the judge should not only have technical knowledge but moreover an artistic feeling for harmony of music and movement of the horse. My explanations should encourage you to be another of our ringside participants. Let us be one in our love for the horse and our celebration of his wonderful potential.

What you are seeing now is the result of a hard work on a long way of horse training—a relationship of rider and horse translated into motion. Let the fresh wind of competition blow through your arena and enjoy the Kur.

Chapter 1
The Musical Freestyle

*The rider is to create and ride from memory an original
ride which shows his horse to its best advantage. In the
Free Style Ride creativity and artistic presentation as well
as technical execution will be considered.*
—AHSA Definition from the **Rule Book**

This simple definition describes one of the fastest developing areas of competition in equestrian sport, the musical freestyle, sometimes referred to as a *kür*. It's not hard to understand why. The sight of a horse and rider dancing their way through choreography of technical craftsmanship set to music is beautiful and inspiring, a true celebration of harmony between man and the horse. There is a magical quality to it.

The value of the musical freestyle to the sport of dressage cannot be underestimated. It does for dressage what ice dancing has done for skating, in bringing new spectators to the sport. Where all too frequently the spectators at a dressage competition were mostly family, grooms, and other participants, we now see non-horse spectators flocking to shows and taking a great interest in musical freestyle rides. With the growing popularity of these rides, classes are now performed beginning with First Level through Grand Prix.

To gain a better understanding of the requirements for this musical performance, let's look closely at dictionary definitions:

> **Free:** Not confined to the usual rules or
> patterns—in a free manner. Not subject

to restraint, at liberty, independent, self-deciding, without obstruction, without charge, unconfined. Able to move in any direction.

Style: A manner of doing, a distinctive or especially admired manner of expressing thought. A distinctive or characteristic manner. Overall excellence, skill, or grace in performance.

Freestyle: Sports not limited to a specified style, pattern of movement, etc.

These definitions suggest how innovative the horse and rider team can and should be. The requirements in musical freestyle competition emphasize technical skills, superb music and choreography, and artistic presentation. The demands placed on the horse are for the gaits, strength, and obedience. When there is a weakness in a ride, one or more of these seven elements is lacking.

To gain a good idea of just what is expected from competitors in the sport, take a look at the official score sheets found in the back of this book. In addition, official score sheets for First, Second and Third Levels may be purchased from the United States Dressage Federation, Inc. P.O. Box 80668, Lincoln, NE 68501. For Fourth, Intermediate, and Grand Prix Levels, contact the American Horse Shows Association, Inc., 220 East 42nd Street, New York, NY 10017-5806. Within each level, there are compulsory movements to be performed but the figures may be performed in any order.

An interesting note about the word *kür*, which is also used to refer to this musical performance. Although the word has been used in this context for a long time, its derivation seems to be a mystery. The origin is German but German dictionaries list nothing related to either horses or music: courting, love, teaching, health, to elect or to exercise at discretion. Perhaps it evolves from this last definition in some way. In this book, though, I use the term musical freestyle as it is used by the USDF and AHSA.

It must be noted at the outset that there is no compromise of classical dressage in the art of musical freestyle by setting the movements to music. Consider the following:

1. An extended trot is a beautiful sight to see.

2. A *correct* extended trot is not only beautiful but also inspirational.

3. A *correct* extended trot *set to music* is not only beautiful and inspirational, it is a celebration for the senses of seeing, hearing and *feeling*.

It is as important in the freestyle as in the regular tests that the transitions and movements of the performance be correct and true.

There has been much discussion concerning the pro's and con's of having freestyles in the lower levels of dressage. To my mind, there is no question about it: we need the lower level freestyles! To me, suggesting they are not necessary or useful is like suggesting, "Why not eliminate anything below Prix St. George?" or, "Why not eliminate minor league baseball?" The reasons are obvious:

1. Musical freestyle has to be learned by degree of difficulty, just as the compulsory tests. You cannot start at the top.

2. The lower level riders are in the process of learning *now;* they are the Grand Prix riders of the future.

3. Performance and competition in the lower levels helps the sport to grow and creates more interest for riders and spectators.

Without meaning to sound critical, I must say that I see Grand Prix level freestyles performed with only a Training level ability in the musical or artistic portions of the ride. These riders make obvious mistakes: the music is off or they lose artistic value by not taking advantage of letting variations in the music put emphasis on different movements. There are many things about the freestyle that have to be learned gradually at different levels in the same way that technical riding execution is learned with the horse in a progressive manner.

To be able to create a musical freestyle ride, you do not have to be greatly concerned about complex theories of music. You do not even have to be particularly musical to get a great deal of enjoyment from creating a musical ride with your horse. While it would be super if you were able to go to a musical show and then come home and play all the tunes, have absolute pitch, and recognize the note A when you hear it, it is not a requirement for creating a freestyle ride. No one can listen to a piece of special music without sooner or later being invaded, as it were, by the beat. The music takes hold with snapping fingers, tapping feet, or clapping hands. If music can do this to you, you have the ability to be a freestyle rider.

And what about your horse? Does it naturally have the ability to dance? The whole question of "Do animals dance?" is an interesting one. Many primitive peoples take for granted the correspondence between the movements of animals and the choreography of dance; this notion is often incorporated into their own dances by imitation. Animals often seem to be performing dances when they are wooing a prospective mate (or fighting over one).

Most people, however, would reject this as simply a projection of a strictly human activity onto animals. Your horse cannot dance with you in the same way that another human would. Much of the performance of the musical freestyle reflects adapting the music and choreography to the horse, rather than the other way around.

One thing is clear, however: your horse will respond to the musical freestyle in a way you have probably never felt before. It may be that because you as rider-director are responding to either the *feeling* the music gives you and the horse follows, or because your rhythm becomes more consistent while you ride to music, but there is no doubt that there is a visable effect on the horse. This is one of the joys you have awaiting you as you learn more about the musical freestyle.

Chapter 2
Basic Principles in Musical Freestyle

Before we begin to learn how to choreograph and orchestrate a freestyle ride, it's important to understand a few of the underlying principles we'll be working with. You don't have to be a musical expert but you will need to learn enough to help you select the proper music for your horse and for each segment of your ride.

Let's look first at the three basic gaits of the horse, and then at two important terms used in both music and riding: rhythm and tempo.

The Horse's Gaits

The walk is a gait of four-time rhythm with four distinct hoofbeats. They are heard in every stride as each foot in turn strikes the ground by itself (the sequence is lateral-consecutive) and is never performed in a combination or together with any other foot. A strictly even tempo in four-time must be maintained since, without this, the horse is no longer walking.

The trot is a gait of two-time rhythm on alternate diagonals, with two distinct beats. This gait is the horse's most rhythmical, and should look as though dancing from one diagonal to the other. Regularity, elasticity, and impulsion originate from a supple back and engaged hind quarters.

The canter is a gait of three-time rhythm in which three hoofbeats and a period of suspension occur to each stride. When this three-time cadence is lost, the essense of a pure canter becomes faulty either through lack of energy of the horse, or lack of influence by his rider. A quality canter will be light and regular, with the ability to maintain a natural balance, and the horse is straight from head to tail.

Rhythm

The order of the foot falls. Simply the "beat" of the gait (Walk: 4-beat; Trot: 2-beat, Canter: 3-beat).
**—Rule Book,
American Horse Shows Association, Inc.**

Rhythm denotes the regularity of steps. The rhythm of the horse is the relative time of the length of successive foot falls. . . A regular flow of action. Rhythm is part of music.

Rhythm is the great organizer of all the ingredients in the art of riding, the most persuasive, and most powerful element.

The rhythm denotes the regularity of the steps in all three gaits: even or uneven. Rhythm is a regular or measured flow of the horse's action. The goal of good riding is to maintain an even rhythm relative to each gait of the horse. If the horse is naturally well balanced, and the rider maintains the relaxation, the horse will be able to keep a good rhythm.

Few horses have "built-in" rhythm, and it is something which is really up to the rider to maintain. Constant correction in the early stages of training is essential to establish this basic principle of riding.

The two gaits at which the rhythm is most frequently at fault are the trot and canter. The horse must be allowed to learn to control his legs at a slower, more relaxed speed. In this manner, you will be able to improve the rhythm of the steps which should blend smoothly together. You, the rider, must concentrate on the rhythm required, 1-2 for trot, and 1-2-3 for the canter, and 1-2-3-4 for the walk. If you like, count out loud, or do some work on a hard surface; this will enable you to hear the beat of the foot falls.

The correct rhythm for a horse is controlled by a regular beat. The rider needs to think about keeping every stride the same if the horse is not particularly well coordinated. If the rider has no sense of rhythm, it can be developed by counting as mentioned before, or by singing or whistling while riding. Once an even rhythm can be maintained by the horse, it will become more balanced, and able to use itself more efficiently.

The freestyle rider must develop an association between:

- Feeling the rhythm on the horse, constant and consistent, and

- Hearing the rhythm in the music, listening, and analyzing.

There are three types of rhythm in music that can help differentiate the rhythm of the horse:

- Metrical rhythm. The rhythm is said to be metrical when characterized by equality and regularity. Horses have metrical rhythm as it emphasizes the use of the big muscles in large, free, regular motions.

- Syncopated rhythm. Syncopated rhythm is a disturbance of the normal meter that changes the length of the rhythmic cluster.

- Measured rhythm. This type has no regular recurring beat, the pace is set according to the impulses of the moment to what it wants to do or say, such as in a Gregorian chant.

Remember, rhythm denotes the regularity of the steps, even or uneven. It is only the length of stride that changes and, of great importance, the rhythm must remain the same in all tempos. Rhythm of movement is the music of riding.

You will be able to move proficiently to music when you understand the meaning and relationship of rhythm and tempo.

Tempo

TEMPO is the rate of repetition of the rhythm. It is not synonymous with speed (Speed—miles per hour—can be produced either by an increase in tempo or a lengthening of the strides.)

**—Rule Book,
American Horse Shows Association, Inc.**

Tempo means time, measure or beat of any rhythmical motion. Tempo refers to the speed of the beat. A steady, even tempo is necessary to preserve the rhythmical swing of the horse.

Tempo is the *measure of speed,* and pertains to the degrees of slow, moderate, and fast. A steady, even tempo is necessary to preserve the rhythmical swing of the horse.

At the same time, however, tempo is determined by the character and mood of the horse. By this I mean changes in tempo can occur from slow to fast by a variation in diet, weather, footing, and health of the horse. If these variations happen, the rider must feel and make the necessary adjustments to the correct tempo. This is one of the most important factors in an effective performance of a musical freestyle.

Tempo, as the rate of speed or movement, is the rate of repetition of the rhythm. It depends on the horse's make-up and temperament. No matter what the individualized tempo of the horse, it must stay the same while going around the arena, into corners, moving laterally across the ring and throughout circles. The horse must not speed up or slow down at any given gait. It is the rider's responsibility to make corrections necessary to maintain a true tempo.

For tempo, there are commonly employed musical terms for degrees of fast and slow. Traditionally (but not always) the terminology is given in Italian. Here are a few from slowest to fastest. Compare: where do you think your horse fits in?

Largo—very slow and broad
Adaigo—very slow
Lento—slow
Andante—"walking" tempo; implies a slow steady
           movement
Moderato—moderate tempo
Allegro—quick, fast
Vivace—spirited
Presto—very fast

As you can see, tempo terms have a positive meaning, but are open to various individual interpretations as each horse will have its own measure of speed, or tempo.

There are also relationships between tempo terms frequently used that are predominately descriptive, but convey the "character" of the horse:

Maestoso—majestically, slow to moderate tempo
Tranquillo—calmly
Grazioso—gracefully
Animato—animated
Scherzoso—in a jesting, playful manner
Con fuoco—with fire; fast or very fast tempo
Con brio—brisk, lively

So, throughout this book, when we use the word tempo, it can apply to both the horse and the music.

Rhythm and *tempo*, though obviously intimately interrelated, are never-the-less independent variables. Both are very important, and you must have a clear perception of each before attempting to choreograph and orchestrate your musical freestyle ride.

Chapter 3
A Little Music Theory

I am not going to try to teach you to read music or even make you feel it is necessary to read music to create a musical freestyle. There are many good books on music theory alone. My goal is to teach you to relate music to the rhythms of the horse. However, in the process of learning to time the horse and music and arrive at the beats per minute, you will eventually be confronted with basic music terms, especially as you become more deeply involved working with the musical freestyle. This little music theory lesson may take away some of the mystery of the correlation between the horse's gaits and music. The illustrations of very basic music theory will help you to read the rhythm patterns that we encounter in music that are identical to the three rhythms of the horse.

What is a Beat?

Many years ago military leaders determined that when a soldier was marching and took a full step, or pace (i.e., left, right, left), he would cover approximately one yard. To keep a consistent cadence (or beat) they first used drums with a heavy emphasis on the "down-beat" or each time the left foot hit the ground. This showed that a steady cadence or drum beat of 130 (down) beats per minute would have them cover one mile in approximately 13½ minutes. Hence, most march music is played at 130 beats per minute. If you have ever marched in a parade, you can recall counting "left, left, left-right-left," putting the emphasis on the left foot to coincide with the downbeats of the bass drum.

This was the practical use of downbeats per minute. In the freestyle we are faced with a similar problem, but more complex, due to existing variables: horses are of different sizes and individual horses have their own tempo, moving at different downbeats per minute; and horses change their rate of downbeats per minute as they become more collected and developed.

In music, the amount of time a note is held is measured in units and is also called the *beat*. A beat is a regular pulsation. A clock ticks to a regular beat all by itself. Conductors indicate the beat to an orchestra by the up and down movements of their hands.

There are sounds in beat patterns: the two-beat pattern of breathing, heartbeats, tides, skipping, clapping, and, of course, dancing. Adding to all of these are the wonderful sounds of hoof beats, the music to our ears.

Beats can be compared to tapping your foot in an even and steady manner. Look at one foot of your horse in trot. Do you see the tapping? When tapping, two motions are required— down and up, down and up, and so on. Therefore, each beat has two parts or halves: a *downbeat* and an *upbeat*.

Each time you tap your foot (the downbeat), a number is counted starting with one, and each time the toe is raised (the upbeat), the word "and" is said. Try doing as the illustration shows, tapping and counting the downbeat.

Now look at the illustration of the front hooves of the horse: there is the repeat of the tapping—the downbeat and the upbeat.

To come back to the original point: a beat is a regular pulsation. Take a few moments and watch a horse and rider:

> The eye sees the motion of the hoof and impulsively will set the body or foot in motion to imitate and to keep in time.

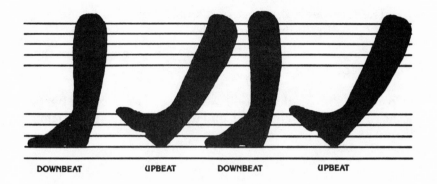

DOWNBEAT   UPBEAT   DOWNBEAT   UPBEAT

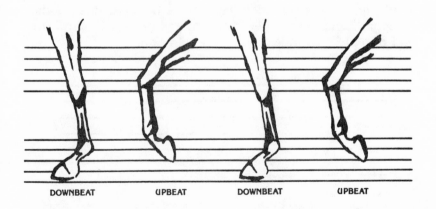

DOWNBEAT   UPBEAT   DOWNBEAT   UPBEAT

The ears listen to the footfalls of the horse's hoofs, striking repeatedly.

The rider feels the beat of his horse with his whole body by following the motion.

The eyes, the ears, and the body are all engaged in the concept of the beat.

To create a musical freestyle, we will need to calculate beats of the movements of the horse, and the beats of the movements of music.

Measure, Bar Lines, and Double Bar Lines

Music is divided into equal parts called measures. On a sheet of music, the distance between two vertical bar lines is the measure. Double bar lines, one thin and one thick, show the end of a piece of music.

BAR LINE   BAR LINE

BAR LINE   BAR LINE   DOUBLE BAR LINE

Note Values

The time intended for a tone to sound is indicated by the shape and color of the written note and by additional stems, flags, and dots which may be attached to the note. The whole note is the basic value against which all other values are measured. The following notes show several ways the whole note can be subdivided.

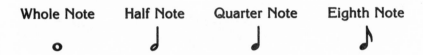

| Whole Note | Half Note | Quarter Note | Eighth Note |

One whole note equals two half notes

$$\mathbf{o} \; = \; \mathbf{d} \; \mathbf{d}$$

One half note equals two quarter notes

$$\mathbf{d} \; = \; \mathbf{J} \; \mathbf{J}$$

One whole note equals four quarter notes

$$\mathbf{o} \; = \; \mathbf{J} \; \mathbf{J} \; \mathbf{J} \; \mathbf{J}$$

One whole note equals eight eighth notes

$$\mathbf{o} \; = \; \mathbf{\flat} \; \mathbf{\flat} \; \mathbf{\flat} \; \mathbf{\flat} \; \mathbf{\flat} \; \mathbf{\flat} \; \mathbf{\flat} \; \mathbf{\flat}$$

A dot after a note (.) adds one count which prolongs the value of a note by half of its original value. For example, a dotted half note (♩.) equals three counts.

Whole Note

(**o**) . . . . This note gets *four* counts.

Dotted Half Note

(♩.) . . . . This note gets *three* counts.

Half Note

(♩) . . . . This note gets *two* counts.

Dotted Quarter Note

(♩.) . . . . This note gets *one and one-half* counts.

Quarter Note

(♩) . . . . This note gets *one* count.

Eighth Note

(♪) . . . . This note gets *one-half* count.

Here is another visual method of comprehending these relationships:

Each note we encounter in music has a definite time value. If you study the illustrations of note values, you will soon be able to compare them to a 12-inch ruler. The ruler is marked in inches with their fractional parts measuring lengths. So it is with music notes measuring lengths indicated by their form.

Time Signatures

A time signature is placed at the beginning of a piece of music. There is a top and bottom number: i.e. 4/4. The top number shows the number of beats (or counts) in each measure. The bottom number shows what kind of note gets one beat.

In $\frac{4}{4}$ time, there are four beats in each measure.

A whole note receives four beats.

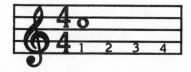

A half note receives two beats.

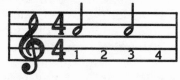

A quarter note receives one beat.

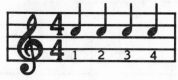

The walk is a four-beat movement.

In  time, there are two beats in each measure, and each quarter note gets one beat.

The trot is a two-beat movement.

In **3/4** time, there are three beats in each measure and each quarter note gets one beat.

The canter is a three-beat movement.

To sum up this brief music theory lesson, remember that each note has a definite length of time or beat, just as each footfall of a horse can be measured for length of time or number of beats.

Compare these illustrations with the rhythms of the horse: 2 beats for the trot, 3 beats for the canter, and 4 beats for the walk. This will appear again, and again throughout this book as it is part of the basic theory for counting beats per minute.

The Music Rhythms of the Horse

The Trot Rhythm of the Horse

The Canter Rhythm of the Horse

The Walk Rhythm of the Horse

Phrases

The word *phrase* is an important word in music. Understanding phrasing can make a significant difference in the quality of your tape for a musical freestyle.

Think of music as language. When we express our thoughts in spoken language, we do it by using *words*. To convey our feelings in *music*, we use *tones* instead of *words*. Since music is divided into logical sections, it can be compared to a sentence in a speech, or equivalent to punctuation marks in a written language. Just as a sentence is divided by commas, colons, and so forth into smaller parts of speech (phrases and clauses), a musical sentence is divided by measured movements into phrases. When we hear a story, we listen sentence by sentence; when we listen to music, we listen phrase by phrase. Hence, musical sentences are called *phrases*. In short, phrasing is punctuation applied to music.

In music, a phrase is a short musical thought at least two, but typically four measures, in length. A phrase is the natural division of a melody. Only when the notes are arranged into musical sentences do they take on a definite meaning, or phrase.

Like any language, music is a combination of phrases. If you tell a story or recite poetry, you do not stop in the middle or part way through a phrase. Music will have the same effect if you stop and do not finish a musical phrase. This holds true with or without the words. Variations in music and the ending of musical phrases can be used as a signal to indicate a transition or change in movements or gaits.

The concept of phrasing will be important as you begin to select and edit the music for your freestyle ride. It will allow you to develop a flowing, fluent ride without abrupt stops that leave your audience hanging.

Chapter 4
Getting Started

How to Determine and Use Beats Per Minute

Beats per minute is the key to uniting the components for the musical freestyle. Using beats per minute as your guide, you will learn to time the horse and music, and to select the correct music for each segment of the horse's gaits. Horses cannot "dance" with you, not in the same manner as a human, so by using this theory you will *adapt the music to the horse.* This is what will give the delightful feeling of dancing together.

When I use the word *beat,* I want you to think specifically of the *downbeat.* This is the beat where everything starts. Visualize a conductor of an orchestra, baton raised, all musician's eyes are on him as he brings *down* the baton emphatically on the first note or *downbeat* and the orchestra plays.

As the conductor moves the baton, there is always one emphatic *downbeat* repeated at even intervals. This is the tempo, or the measure of speed. When you tap your foot or clap your hands to music, you almost unknowingly go to emphasizing the heavy downbeat.

Lawrence Welk is often kidded about his distinctive method of starting the band by tapping his foot, moving his hands up and down and saying, "A One and A Two, and A One and A Two." What he was actually doing was accurately setting a tempo for very danceable music. To further analyze this little ritual of his, I will put the heavy emphasis or downbeat: "A ONE and a TWO and a ONE and a TWO." You can readily see where the downbeat fits with the upbeat in between ("and a"). Try this by moving your arm up and down as a conductor does with the downbeat emphasized and the upbeat in between.

Before you begin to choreograph and orchestrate your ride, you need a clear perception of the *three basic gaits of the horse.* Next we'll learn to count the rate of speed, the tempo of each of the horse's gaits. First, though, let's look at the various timing tools used for this.

Timers

How you keep time will be a matter of preference. Before making a large investment in all of the various time keepers, do some shopping where you can handle and try out the timer to select the one most suitable for your needs.

You can probably go right to work and do well with the wrist watch on your arm if it has a second hand, or even a simple household clock with a second hand. However, as you become more involved in working with the musical freestyle, the more sophisticated equipment will be an asset. Just as the carpenter needs a variety of tools for his trade, the person involved with the musical freestyle needs to have instruments to help make a finished product. I will describe the three basic timers, but you will find modified versions.

Metronome

A metronome is a timepiece invented in the nineteenth century. This timepiece makes a ticking sound for any speed at which it is set, from one to over 200 beats a minute. It has a clockwork device with an inverted pendulum that beats time at a rate determined by the position of a sliding weight on the pendulum.

Hand wind-up types of metronomes produce audible sounds, while an electrical one flashes light and intermittent sounds at any desired musical speed. Both are especially useful to help a person working with music maintain a regular tempo. The metronome setting indicates the exact number of beats per minute and will show the tempo precisely.

Modern metronomes come in pocket size, with batteries, quartz movements, earphone jacks, and switch selections that let you hear the beat and see it on a red LED (light emitting diode). Or, you can just rely on the flashing LED, without sound. The electronic metronome is the best investment because it operates in any position, and is unlikely to have an uneven beat.

Kitchen Timer

A kitchen timer is another instrument that is very useful when working with horses and music. The timer can be used for "count down" to check a ride for length of time required. Some you can also use as a stopwatch to check the tempo of the horse.

It is best to use a battery operated timer because of accuracy. There are spring driven ones, but they are not accurate below a minute for timing. I prefer the electronic kitchen timer because of the audible signal at the end of the interval of time for which it is set. The large dial and digital read-out numbers are great for rapid reading. The particular timer that I use is also a clock when not being used for timing.

The electronic kitchen timer is an excellent tool for a judge or scribe to use primarily because it can be preset to the time allowed for a ride. When the exact time is up, the bell will ring, and give you east-to-read digital numbers and then continue to read out in minutes and seconds the overtime of the ride.

Stopwatch

A stopwatch is made to account for elapsed time in split seconds, seconds, minutes or, in some instances, hours. It has a hand that can be started and stopped at will by pressing a small button on the edge of the watch. There are spring wound as well as elaborate electronic stop watches. There are also special ones made for the various sporting events, such as auto racing, horse racing, and boxing. All are quite function in timing beats per minute of the horse.

The spring wound stop watch is usually equipped with a split second hand, second hand and minute hand. By operating the two buttons, you can start, stop, continue or re-set to zero. Some of the newer "chronograph" watches are equipped with features to be used for elapsed time. My favorite is an oversized stop-watch because it fits in the palm of my hand and I can press the on-off button while keeping my eyes on the horse. I want the exact timing to start with the downbeat of the horse's hoof. As an added feature, the large readout numbers are easily visible at a glance. Each watch has its own general instructions, but all are capable of timing elapsed time (as of a race), with various degrees of accuracy depending on the quality.

The electronic advances have made it possible to own an electronic timer at a modest price.

Counting the Beats Per Minute

To determine the beats per minute of your horse, you will need a stop watch or a watch with a second hand, and an unmounted helper who is familiar with horse gaits. Horses differ in their tempo when starting to work. I prefer the horse not be warmed up before timing as it will give me a true picture of the attitude and tempo of the horse. Some horses maintain the same tempo coming out of the stall, going to work and continuing into collection. Then there is the stable mate who will start working in a hurried frenzy, then settle into a stable tempo. A third type of horse will be very sluggish to start and have to be pushed into the correct tempo. Twenty minutes is the average time needed to determine the beats per minute of a horse.

The average category of beats per minute for each gait are:

Walk	50 to 66	Beats Per Minute
Passage	60 to 64	Beats Per Minute
Trot	76 to 88	Beats Per Minute
Canter	96 to 108	Beats Per Minute

A horse can still be correct if it is an exception to this beats-per-minute listing.

Timing the horse and timing the music are very similar to taking a person's pulse. When a nurse or doctor checks the pulse, they watch the second hand of a watch and determine how many times the heart beats in one minute. This same method is used to determine the beats per minute of a horse. I use the inside front leg to act as a guide to determine the beats per minute of all gaits.

It will be necessary to re-time your findings several times to ensure accuracy. The walk especially needs to be timed at the beginning of the work and after a trot or canter; this is the difficult gait. If the horse is stiff or an older one, the walk will become more free with loosening work. After you have re-checked your beats per minute several times, you will have the normal average for that horse at the particular gait. Write down the numbers for the beats per minute for each time you time a gait. It will look like this: Trot - 88/88/80/80/80. These figures indicate the horse started to work fast, but it is obvious that the most correct tempo number is 80. Continue to time each gait until the horse settles into one number which will be the consistent beats per minute.

It might be helpful to have your unmounted helper count the beats per minute of your horse while you are having a lesson, working with your instructor to make certain your horse is in its true working gaits.

You will be amazed after working with the music how inconsistent a horse can be in its tempo. You, as the rider, will become the disciplinarian of the tempo. Some horses need correction often, so using the music as your guide will better your whole riding program.

There is another method to this that I ought to mention here. Using a video cassette recorder to make a tape of all three gaits can help you count the beats per minute without the extra helper. In addition, you can use this tape later when you have selected music to see how well it matches your horse's gaits.

Now let's look at all three gaits and count the beats per minute for each. We'll begin with the trot as it is perhaps the easiest to use and understand how this works.

The Trot

Per: American Horse Shows Association Rule Book

1. The Trot is a pace of "two time" on alternate diagonal legs (near fore and right hind leg and vice versa) separated by a moment of suspension.

2. The Trot always with free, active and regular steps should be moved into without hesitation.

3. The quality of the Trot is judged by the general impression, the regularity and elasticity of the steps · originated from a supple back and well engaged hind quarters · and by the ability of maintaining the same rhythm and natural balance even after transition from one trot to another.

To determine the beats per minute of the horse at a trot, the person with a stop watch must be at a good vantage point, usually in the arena, to watch the movement of the horse's legs. The horse will be asked to work to the left hand. (Since so many things we do with the horse are done from the left—bridling, mounting, leading—I always start to the left.) The person timing will first practice just counting and watching every time the left front foot strikes the ground. Then, using the stop watch, the timer counts how many times the left front foot strikes the ground in one minute. This number is the beats per minute of the trot. The most common range for the trot is 76 to 88 beats per minute.

Again, check the beats per minute several times to ensure accuracy. I cannot stress this point enough because you will find it to be extremely important to all gaits. As a horse changes, physically and athletically, the number of beats per minute could possibly change. If that happens, it is just a matter of checking the tempo again.

Keep in mind that what you are doing is determining the tempo, or time, which will be the basis for bringing together all of the components for a successful freestyle to music. Remember, the trot is one downbeat, and one up beat. The emphasis is only on the down beat: **down**—up—**down**—up.

The Walk

Per: American Horse Shows Association Rule Book

1. The Walk is a marching pace in which the footfalls of the horse's feet follow one another in "four-time," well marked and maintained in all work at the Walk.

2. When the four beats cease to be distinctly marked, even and regular the Walk is disunited or broken.

3. It is at the pace of Walk that the imperfections of Dressage are most evident. This is also the reason why a horse should not be asked to walk "on the bit" at the early stages of his training. A too precipitous collection will not only spoil the Collected Walk but the Medium and the Extended Walk as well.

To determine the beats per minute of the horse at a walk, follow the same procedure as the trot. The walk is a four-beat movement. The horse will have either two or three feet on the ground simultaneously, and no period of suspension as in the canter and trot. When performed with regularity, you will hear four distinct and even footfalls.

As in the trot, the horse will be asked to walk to the left hand. The person timing with a stop watch will count for one minute every time the left front foot strikes the ground. This number is the beats per minute of the walk. The most common range for the walk is 50 to 66 beats per minute.

The Canter

Per: American Horse Shows Association Rule Book

1. The Canter is a pace of three time, where at Canter to the right, for instance, the footfalls follow one another as follows; left hind, left diagonal (simultaneously left fore and right hind), right fore, followed by a movement of suspension with all four feet in the air before the next stride begins.

*2. The Canter always with light, cadenced and regular
strides, should be moved into without hesitation.*

*3. The quality of the Canter is judged by the general im-
pression, the regularity and lightness of the three-time pace
- originated in the acceptance of the bridle with a supple
poll and in the engagement of the hind quarters with an
active hock action - and by the ability of maintaining the
same rhythm and a natural balance even after a transition from one Canter to another. The horse should always
remain straight on straight lines.*

To determine the beats per minute of the horse at a canter,
follow the same procedure as the trot and walk. This gait is a
three-beat movement with each stride separated by a moment
of suspension. The canter is correct when three hoof beats can
be heard and the horse bounds elastically from the ground and
returns to it unchanged.

As with the trot and walk, your helper should watch the left
front foot, counting how many times it strikes the ground in one
minute. The most common range for the canter is 96 to 108
beats per minute.

A Note on Timing Passage and Piaffe

Ideally, passage and piaffe should be in the exact same tempo.
I find it easier to time the passage.

You time the passage exactly as you did the other three gaits.
An interesting note is that the beats per minute of passage will
normally be approximately 20 beats per minute less than the
trot. For example, with a trot of 84 beats per minute, you can
expect the passage to be about 64 beats per minute. The general
range for passage is 60 to 64 beats per minute.

It is each gait's own distinctive rhythmic pattern that can be
translated into music terminology: trot, 2/4 time; canter, 3/4
time; and walk, 4/4 time. These are the rhythms of the horse.

Now that you have a good understanding of timing the beats per minute of the horse, we can proceed with learning the beats per minute of the music and learn how the two will be united. As you will see, the methods of determining the beats per minute of the music is very similar to determining the beats per minute of the horse.

Timing Music

In much the same manner as we learned to time beats per minute of the horse, we will now go through the procedures for timing music. The instructions and terminology for timing music are very similar to that of working with the horse. The materials that you will need are: records or cassettes of the music that are potentially qualified to use for a freestyle ride; a stop watch, a watch with a second hand, or a metronome; and pencil and paper.

When first selecting music for a freestyle, try to keep it simple, non-vocal, and music that you are familiar with. A heavy emphatic downbeat will be your best helper to start with.

Instead of watching the horse's hoof strike the ground for the downbeat as we did in timing beats per minute of the horse, listen and tap your foot to the rhythm of music to determine the beats per minute. Again, we are measuring the speed of the music, or the tempo.

Remember what I said before: the downbeat is where everything starts. You watched and timed the downbeats of the horse's three rhythms, which have parallel existence to music. You count the downbeat of the music to determine the beats per minute of the music.

German music is often a good choice for learning to time music because of the "oom-pah and oom-pah, pah-pah." This music usually has a strong bass downbeat, followed by a light after beat. It makes you want to tap or clap on the downbeat. A heavy downbeat in the music is advantageous since it strongly encourages the rider to coordinate the rhythm of the horse and movement with the music.

I suggest starting by playing either a polka or a march, try-ing to listen for the downbeat. Tap your foot and clap your hands with the downbeat of the music. Just as you watched your horse at a trot, tap your foot in the same manner. All music has a pro-minent downbeat, but some types are a little harder to distinguish. After some practice, though, you will be able to tap out and hear the music with even a more difficult beat.

There are two ways to measure the tempo of the music. One way is to use the stop watch or a watch with a second hand. I recommend trying this method first because it will make you more adept at determining the beats per minute.

A second method is to use a metronome, either a hand wind-up type or the electronic kind. As you listen to the music, keep adjusting the metronome until you have two matching downbeats, the downbeat of the music and the downbeat of the metronome. This will be the beats per minute. When you are using the metronome to check the tempo, you will soon recognize if the beat is short or long. It requires practice and concentration to coordinate the beat of the metronome and the music.

There is another way to make good use of the metronome in selecting music. If you have a lot of music to time, and are looking especially for a tune with a particular tempo (for ex-ample, you need music at 80 beats per minute), set the metronome at 80 beats per minute. You can be busy with other chores while the tape or record and metronome are on. As soon as a musical tune is played in the tempo that you have set on the metronome, you will hear the two matching downbeats. Make a note of the song and tempo for future reference.

Once you master feeling and hearing the downbeat of the music, time it for one minute; this will be the beats per minute of the music.

Another way to time the music (and the horse) is to use a procedure similar to the way a doctor or nurse checks the pulse. To save time, they check the beats of the pulse for ten seconds and multiply by six to get the pulse reading for one minute. I use a fifteen second reading and multiply by four, especially when it is a short piece of music and timing for a full minute is difficult or impossible.

Chapter 5
Working with Music

Selecting the Music

Selecting the music for a freestyle is a time-consuming job, but it can also be a very pleasant adventure. Just don't start this project with only weeks to go before your competition or it will end up being a big frustration. You should plan on approximately 80 hours of work from start to finish, to go into preparing the choreography, the music, and the cassette tape.

I find that, in general, it makes no difference if you develop the ride for a musical freestyle or select the music first. You will be working with each portion independently to begin with, and it's a good idea to work on both simultaneously. There's certainly plenty to be done, so while you work on the technical side of your program with the horse, you should also be listening to and timing a lot of music.

It's a good idea to keep it simple when you first start out. I recommend using music that you are familiar with in the beginning, music that you have timed and found to have the correct beats per minute for your horse at all three gaits. In addition, the music should make you feel comfortable, happy, and very much in a "togetherness" with your horse.

Styles of Music

The ultimate success of your freestyle ride is through the proper selection of music and beats per minute for your horse's gaits. And there is such a wide range of styles of music to choose from!

In music, style refers to a characteristic way of using melody, rhythm, tone, color, dynamics, harmony, texture, and form. Music such as the march, the waltz, jazz, rock, patriotic, and so on, all have their own basic plans. The particular way these elements are combined results in a total sound that is distinctive or unique.

Folk Music

Some of our most beautiful music came, not as you might suppose, from the pens of famous composers but from the folk tunes which have come down to us from generation to generation. This folk-music tells of human experiences and, for this reason, there are many varieties of folk songs. There are work songs, love songs, cradle songs, drinking songs, war songs, and on and on.

Because of its charming simplicity, folk music from every nation, region, and group is enjoyed by people from other nations and walks of life because it deals with universal human experiences. Many folk tunes will endure forever as masterpieces of melody. Folk music is indigenous to a particular region or people because it reflects the musical preferences of that people or region.

The term folk music covers a variety of types of music such as dixieland, country western, and all nationalities. With its simplicity, melodic patterns and even tempo, folk music is worth investigating for your ride, especially the dance forms. Dance music often shows the different national styles very clearly. With an understanding of these national "styles," you will be able to be more precise in planning and selecting music for the freestyle when you want to express a mood.

You will also find that national musical traits influence style. French music is likely to be of a rhythmic, light beat, and sophisticated. German music is apt to be vigorous, with sturdy rhythm, and thick texture. On the other hand, Russian music is likely to go to extremes of loud, soft, fast and slow, and to have mixed and less common meters. Italian music is usually vital, rhythmic, with a more marked beat, emphasis on melody, and the beauty of the voice. Selected jazz records are particularly suitable for the musical freestyle ride because most of it utilizes two-beat or 2/4 time.

Latin Music

Latin music is beautiful to ride to, but difficult to find where it is recorded without changes in the tempo. Your best chance of finding this would be recordings by smaller orchestras that would not be prone to use symphonic arrangements with deliberate unsteadiness of tempo.

Ragtime

Ragtime is not quite like any other American style of music. The music emerged in the 1890's and was generally assumed to have been born in the South. Although the geographical origins of ragtime are uncertain, both Chicago and St. Louis are the forerunners.

The ragtime music rhythm pattern accents are in unexpected places which are very odd, electrifying. This is called syncopated. Because ragtime music is basically piano music, the left hand keeps a regularly accented bass beat while the right hand decorates the tune with runs and syncopation. Written in 2/4 time with crisp enunciation, this type of music is especially suited for a horse in trot.

The ragtime piano music of Scott Joplin has been popular with musical freestyle riders and will undoubtedly be with us for a long time.

The march is one of the major sources of ragtime composition, as found in titles such as "March and Two-Step," "Honolulu Ragtime Patrol," "March a la Ragtime," and many more with tempo indications ("tempo di Marcia"). Therefore, the rag and the march share common ground providing music in 2/4 time. It is the rhythmic impulse of ragtime through its characteristic "swing" that has made its impact on being used for musical freestyle riding.

American Modern Music

American music has been greatly accepted as an accompaniment vehicle for sporting events. This form of music is an evolution of sounds with roots in the classics, African, primitive, European, and Asian folk music. When you stop to consider it, American music is not unlike the American people in the make-up from many sources.

When the music has a strong moving beat, "ear-pleasing" harmony and a melody that lingers with you, it has a tendency to be played over and over, and becomes a "hit" song. Some of these "hit" songs become so popular they never go out of style. At this point, they are affectionately referred to as "standards." The standards have a very strong appeal to many people of different backgrounds. Musicians, whether they are playing on the Riviera, aboard a Scandinavian cruise ship, in a New York supper club, or in a private club in Instanbul, are often asked to play standards such as "Misty," "Stardust," "Bill Bailey," "Alley-Cat," and "New York, New York."

These are standards that span about fifty years of American music, that have become internationally loved and will continue for ages. Why? Each is melodic, has feeling, a great beat, and reminds us all of some precious time in our lives.

In most popular types of modern music such as jazz, swing, rock, western, and disco, the tempo generally remains the same throughout a tune; the beat is steady, almost unchanging. This distinctive feature makes it especially suitable for "dancing with your horse." Once the beat is established, you can rely on the "tick-tock" tempo.

Another comparison that can be made is between the popular music musicians' and the symphonic musicians' need to observe the tempo. The musicians that play popular music usually don't rely on a conductor since once a beat is established, it doesn't change. In symphonic music, though, the beat changes often. Symphony musicians need to keep their eyes focusing between their music and the conductor so they can stay with the beat.

We cannot forget in the strictest sense of the word, good country and western music. It is also truly American not limited to any age bracket or any class of people.

Other Styles of Music

Frequently, the person new to musical freestyles assumes that because dressage is "classical," only classical music can be used. This is definitely not so! In fact, classical music may be the most difficult to use successfully.

Classical music is great to listen to if you have the time, and time it will take to listen to the hours necessary to find enough passages with the needed tempo. Because of the ever-changing tempos and dead space, classical music is the most difficult to make into a musical interpretation for the freestyle ride.

Novelty music has been used with fun and success, with "Elephant Walk," and "Mame" as examples. If the tempo is correct, and the mood or theme suitable, they can be impressive to use.

You might also consider half-time music, although it does take a good listening ear and sense of rhythm to follow. For example, let's assume using music that is 120 beats per minute. The horse will be at 60 peats per minute (at the walk or passage), so the heavy downbeat will fall only every other stride. The horse would be at half the tempo of the music. Or put another way, the music is playing double-time, double the tempo of the horse. The Queen's Guards in England parade at half-time which is very regal but can be difficult for a beginner.

The walk of the horse offers another interesting possibility for the music selection. Because in the walk each foot strikes the ground separately (no two feet strike at the same time), you can double the beats per minute in the music. It works like this: suppose your horse is at 52 beats per minute at the walk. You double the music to 104 beats per minute. A horse at 104 beats per minute would have a downbeat as each foot strikes the ground:

1	2	**3**	4	&	**1**	2	**3**	4
Down	Down	**Down**	Down		**Down**	Down	**Down**	Down

Using the double time of music at 104 beats per minute will really project the sense that the horse is marching as each foot strikes the ground with a matching beat of music.

Each horse and rider combination is different. Double time will be workable and comfortable for some, while for others it is perturbing, almost as if the music is overpowering.

An interesting fact: frequently the double time of the walk will have the exact beats per minute of the canter. Think of the possibilities that presents for the music selection.

I know there has been much said and written about using vocal music for a musical freestyle ride. In my opinion, there is no reason why some or all vocal music cannot be used. In screening music for selection, you may find some vocal pieces that are quite usable. It is sometimes hard, though, to find music to complement vocal music since the vocals can be distracting. In competition, the person you are trying most to impress is the judge. If the vocal music is distracting to the audience, it will also be so to the judge.

The last style of music I want to mention is fanfare music. This type is great to use for the entrance, and is not timed as part of the ride (we will talk more about entrance music in the chapter on *Choreographing the Ride*). There are many classical pieces that start with a fanfare, and there are also records and tapes of only fanfare music (mostly European). This is music to use as an attention-getter and you need not be concerned with the beats per minute.

When choosing music, reflect first about these three considerations:

1. Can you feel the music and say, "How wonderful it *feels* with my horse?"

2. Do you *like* the music? Music that feels good and in correct tempo is essential but if for any reason a certain type just turns you off, forget it and try something else.

3. Can you present the music? When you find music that feels good and you like it, start thinking in terms of the dazzling presentation you can make with it.

I often ask myself "What do I want from the music?" when applying music to a horse and rider combination, especially when the image and mood do not project what we are looking for. The best way to approach this dilemma is to use a video and study the three gaits of the horse. Give them a grade like, "Super Best," "Next Best," and "Least Best."

Work with a lot of music and try to give the "Super Best" gait nice, light, floating music. For the "Next Best" gait, use music with a more natural tone and feeling. Now, what to do with the "Least Best" gait? I try to use music that gets *behind* the horse and pushes, simulating a lifting feeling. Take extra time with this portion until you see and feel what will be successful and balance out the ride.

When you select your music, there is such a variety and vast amount to choose from that you can select something that is personal and shows continuity between you and your horse and the ride. It isn't necessary to copy another person or limit yourself in any way. There are more than enough standards to enable everyone to use his or her favorite music and in a completely unique and personal way.

Suitability of Music to Horse and Rider

There is one more concept to keep in mind as you listen to and select the music for your freestyle: the suitability of the music to the horse and rider. This is so important that it is considered to be part of the score (look under "Musicality" on the score sheet). What suitability of the music means is that what you *hear* should match what you *see*. The suitable music will enhance the horse by complementing its size, personality, and breed. Ideally, the music will show and match the versatility and athletic prowess of the horse and rider as well as the ingenuity and creativity presented in the ride.

It may seem obvious that the horse has a big role to play in the freestyle but many times it seems to be forgotten. You must consider your horse, your "dancing partner," as you try to unify the music. Certain musical rhythms, styles and patterns will be tailor-made for your horse. Selecting the suitable music to ride to, adding to the appearance of horse and rider, will contribute in large part to a successful freestyle ride.

Music Sources

Most of us have a record or cassette collection. The first source for music should be with what you have on hand. Here again, music can be very costly if you plan on starting with an all-new collection. Choose sources where you won't have to buy, or at least can be obtained at a reduced cost. Here are a few ideas for you.

Friends. In addition to borrowing records and tapes from friends, you can exchange theme music.

Thrift Stores. I have had great luck in thrift stores with price, quality, and selection.

Libraries. If you haven't been to the library for a long time and aren't aware of the music possibilities, you will be pleasantly surprised at the selection.

Flea Markets. Check out your local flea markets: you will find an abundance of old standard music. Keep your eyes open to the boxes under the sellers' tables for the music. Some of my best records came from these private collections.

Garage Sales. Do the same hunting at the garage sales. If there are no records or tapes in sight, you might ask; many proprietors probably hadn't thought about selling their music until then.

Building on your own resources will make it very easy when the time comes for selecting your music. Just be sure to check the surface of used records for scratches and excessive wear.

Listening to Music

Now that you are involved with the musical freestyle of riding, there will be a new *awareness* of all the music that surrounds you. You can, by keeping alert and listening, find some exciting music that is different for you and your horse.

Before, listening was the most common musical activity. Now you need to take the time and opportunity, through listening, to compare and analyze music in order to develop the ability to make judgment on what can be used for your musical freestyle.

Generally speaking, most people are apt to listen to music while doing something else, listening only enough to be merely aware of the music. As you become a *listener,* you will be able to analyze music to the extent of hearing rhythm patterns, phrases, movement, tempo, loud, soft, fast, slow, heavy, light, happy styles of music, mood, theme and very attractive sounds. The enjoyment of music builds through the foundation of listening, and the development of the ability to *hear* music.

Practice timing music so that you can do it quickly if you hear music that sounds like it might be for you and your horse. The best practice way to determine the tempo (beats per minute) of music is to listen to recordings that you are familiar with, and then time it as you did the timing for the horse. When the music contains familiar sounds, particularly rhythmic and melodic, the new *interest* of using music for the freestyle assists motivation and intrigue in what you are about to hear.

All music does not contain distinct patterns. Listen for the accent in the music or the strong downbeat. This is where you can tap your foot, clap your hands, or jog in place to feel the beat. You will be effected by the impulses of the music as well as the movement or the rhythm of the horse.

I keep a stereo radio station turned to music all the time. In addition, the station encourages listeners to call in for the names of recordings being played. Two of my best pieces of music came from the radio station's reference. This can make listening to variations of music an adventure, somewhat like a mystery which gradually resolves itself as you detect music time and tempo.

This discovery method is an exciting, stimulating, and rewarding way *to learn*. Music should be the discovery of musical sound: how you respond to it, what it is really like, and how it is organized. The idea of listening and listening to music is to help you to further your awareness of patterns of sounds.

The Music Library

By analyzing your record or tape collection, you'll make your own music library more functional. This information might be condensed in a card file for convenience. There are a number of ways in which entries can be made on cards. The most practical method I have found is to use a 4x6 card, writing across the top the record or tape number, song title, duration, gait, music type, and in large print in the top right hand corner, the beats per minute.

Record Number	Song Title	Time	Gait	Music Type	BPM 80
7	Lady	3:15	Trot	Cha Cha	
10	Love Makes The World Go Round	2:42	"	Dixie Waltz	
76	Oklahoma	2:50	"	Show Tune	
16	Figaro	2:12	"	Classic	
78	God Bless America	3:05	"	Patriotic I. Berlin	

Record Library Card Sample

A simple way to identify the records and tapes is to purchase some self-adhesive, ¾" diameter labels, and give each of the records a number.

Next determine the beats per minute of each song on the record or tape. Mark the beats per minute on the jacket. Now start to fill in the cards, making a new card for each of the different beats per minute. If you have more than one piece with the same beats per minute, list them on the same card. Eventually you will have a good selection of music to choose from on each card.

On the "Music Library Card" sample, I chose to use 80 beats per minute as this is the most common trot tempo for horses. You can see at a glance the possibilities you have for choosing theme music. It is very difficult for one record or tape to supply the three or four tempo changes that you will need for a ride.

To improve the quality of your music library, do not include songs that have changes in the tempo, excessive vocals, or those of poor quality. Just mark these songs "N/G" (no good) to save time. Then you'll know that you may have only one song on a record that is suitable for a musical ride, but what is listed will be of good quality.

These headings on the cards will serve as criteria as you listen to each recording. Write only in the spaces beneath the heading that names the outstanding characteristics of the music. File the cards numerically by the beats per minute.

Notice that some records and tapes or their jackets show the total playing time for each music selection such as 1:45, 2:25, 2:30, 2:57, etc. This will be of value to you at the time of selecting music for a freestyle ride. The playing time of 1:45 if it were trot music would be ideal for a Fourth and Intermediate Level freestyle ride. Canter music with a playing time of 2:57 would also be valid to use for the same two levels. When the opportunity comes for you to use a particular piece of music with no time provided, start by taking the actual audible time of the whole piece of music.

The heading of music types will vary with notations such as lively, theme forms, Irish Folk, soft walk, Latin, a distinct mood, tone quality, classical, good entrance, instrumental, violin, organ, feelings. These are just samples of ways to describe what your music is and how it projects to your listening ear.

Once you have completed your analysis of the records and tapes, you will have an easy reference file to find every piece of music you have available at any given beats per minute. This will make a wonderful reference library to use over and over again. I go one step further. Using a simple notebook, I list numerically the number of the record or tape, title and recording artist. The reason for doing this is to have a ready reference of individual artist's styles, instrumentation, and orchestration associated with each recording.

The Practice Tape

As you listen to many kinds of music and begin to find selections with the correct beats per minute for all three of your horse's gaits, you should put together a practice tape (a later chapter explains the technical side of taping). The practice tape will include your favorites from what you've been listening to and analyzing. It's a good idea at this point to include a wide variety of styles of music; don't narrow the focus too much.

Start with a 60-minute cassette tape. On Side 1, make the tape to fit your daily riding pattern. For a beginning 30-minute tape, I suggest five minutes of walk music, ten minutes of trot music, ten minutes of canter music, and end with five minutes of walk music.

On Side 2, record three pieces of music, one piece for each gait. Place these in the sequence you expect to do in the ride. Remember the total time is up to five minutes for First through Third Level, and up to six minutes for Fourth through Grand Prix. The advantages this practice tape offers you are the practice of gaits and music transitions with the technical requirements relative to each level's time allotment.

When you ride, you should play the practice tape, using it to help you *feel* the music. It takes time to find the right music to give you that special feeling, and exploring the possibilities now with a practice tape will help you later in your final selections for the freestyle ride.

You should save this practice tape even after you've made your selections for the freestyle since it will contain music in the tempo timed for your horse's correct gaits. It can be very useful for you as a double-check that your horse is moving correctly and, besides, riding to music is fun!

Lungeing to Music

Training on the lunge with music can be an invaluable tool, allowing you to watch the outcome of the tempo of the horse and music. It will give you a wonderful opportunity to watch for yourself the harmony that can take place and to see the image you are trying to project with the music.

You know already that lungeing, when properly used, is a beneficial training technique. Adding the element of music can do two things. First, by using your practice tape with the correct beats per minute for your horse's gaits, you can establish the regularity of gaits; you'll be able to *see* when they are correct. And, by working with music and your horse together, you'll develop a better sense of rhythm and tempo for when you are riding. All three tempos of the horse at the walk, trot and canter while on the lunge must coincide with the tempos of the work under saddle. You can even use the work on the lunge to check what you have determined to be the correct beats per minute for each gait.

Don't be discouraged if it seems difficult at first. It can be tricky to try and lunge a horse and concentrate on the tempo at the same time. But it is a skill that will come with a little practice.

I suggest starting with the trot music because the trot beat is easier to work with. It always seems to go better if you start on the left hand, probably because most things with a horse are done to the left (tacking up, mounting, leading). As you did when you measured the beats per minute of your horse, use the inside front (left) leg as your guide. This is the downbeat of the horse and you want to make sure the horse maintains the 1–2 rhythm of the trot.

It will be very helpful for you to march or jog in place in time with the horse. As you keep in time with the horse, listen to the music: are you both in time? *You* are the director of the tempo. If the horse's tempo changes, speeding up or slowing down, you must increase or decrease the tempo of the horse to match the tempo of the music.

Now is probably a good time for a word about impulsion: it is always important not to confuse impulsion with just speeding up but very important when working with music. The horse should take longer steps, not simply quicken. Working with music on the lunge can be a tremendous help in gauging if your horse is working with proper impulsion. If you selected music with the correct beats per minute, you will be able to tell immediately if the impulsion is off because the gait and music won't match.

The walk can frequently be improved with music on the lunge. The walk has little natural impulsion, but will become more animated and improved as you encourage the four-beat sequence with music. It is especially important at the walk not to work on too small a circle. The horse needs to be encouraged to have as free and long a stride as possible by influencing the movement of the horse's hind legs.

With the trot, use the horse's inside front leg as your guide, tapping your foot in time, **1-2-3-4, 1-2-3-4**. Because the trot is a two-beat gait, with the horse moving from diagonal to diagonal pairs of legs, the downbeat must be one of two beats. But in the walk, with its four-beat sequence, the downbeat could be one of four: **1-2-3-4**, or **1-2-3-4** or **1-2-3-4** or **1-2-3-4**. You still use the horse's inside front leg as your guide. Music in 4/4 time will be very correct.

The canter work follows in the same fashion. Begin your canter music, watch the horse's foreleg, and count out the three beats: **1-2-3, 1-2-3**. The first beat will always be the timing and leading foreleg.

Lungeing to music with your horse can be a pleasant diversion from your regular training program. It can also be one of the quickest ways to begin to really *feel* the music, and to learn control of tempo.

Chapter 6
Creating Your Musical Freestyle Ride

Having worked with beginners, intermediate and well-experienced riders in the process of teaching the procedures involved in creating a musical freestyle, I know that all are often overwhelmed by the magnitude of the task. Regardless of their riding experience or musical training, they just don't know where to start. From my experience in teaching this method, I can assure you that whether you are a rider of little or great experience, you *will* reach the point where it comes together and gives you many hours of enjoyment, in either practice or competition, in "dancing with your horse."

The key to all this is to have a plan that suits you and your horse. The plan includes three elements:

- Music selection
- Choreography
- Recording and editing

While we look in this book at each of these elements separately, in actual practice you are working on all three simultaneously; they are interwoven in that sense.

There are two different methods that can be used in developing the freestyle ride, one of which will be right for you. They are:

1. Start by selecting the music first by choosing your "theme." This tends to work better for rides in the lower levels because there are fewer compulsory movements to be shown. For levels First through Third the total ride time permitted is five minutes. Stay simple with the music if this will be your first attempt at making a cassette tape for a musical freestyle ride. Planning the music program in writing first will help you get started. Try this sample and adapt your music and times in the same places.

Theme — BIG BAND

RECORD #	GAIT AND NAME OF MUSIC			TIME
000	TROT ·	Name of music	(use total piece)	2:00
000	WALK ·	Name of music	(start at beginning)	1:10
000	CANTER ·	Name of music	(use total piece)	1:45
			Total Ride Time	4:55

Making use of existing musical pieces simplifies the recording job by having only two places to piece the music. There is adequate time in the music to perform the compulsory movements for the three gaits.

2. Plan your ride first, and then edit and refine the music to fit the ride. This method works best for rides in the upper levels because of the greater number of required movements.

The total music time needed for Fourth Level and Intermediate rides is 6 minutes. Because of the increased trot and canter work in these two levels (the music times can still be kept simple), allow almost equal time to the trot and canter and less time to the walk compared to levels First through Third. Also, to make these rides a little more interesting, make one more division of the gaits and music as in the example:

FOURTH LEVEL & INTERMEDIATE RIDE

CANTER	1:30
TROT	2:20
WALK	:45
CANTER	<u>1:20</u>
Total Ride Time	<u>5:55</u>

The more times you divide the gaits and music for a ride, the more times you will have to join music. The example above has three music splices to make. This take practice and patience to do, but look how much more interesting the ride–music combination becomes.

Grand Prix rides and music will take more time. The addition of the passage and piaffe requires their own music and creates a new division of times between the walk, trot, and canter. There are numerous ways to arrange the ride and music for a Grand Prix Freestyle. I always first consider the physical and technical ability of the horse and rider in passage because it is the highest and most difficult movement. If this is the first year of showing passage for the horse, it will most likely not be strong enough to use the passage as the high "show-off" part of the ride. Keep the time to about one minute for this horse in passage. The stronger, experienced horse can physically do more and can use it as the soaring part or parts of the ride. The example below shows what I would do with a ride for a horse competent in passage. Remember, the Grand Prix ride is six minutes with a minimum of five minutes and thirty seconds. Now the difficulty will increase to 5 pieces of music needing to be spliced.

GRAND PRIX RIDE

PASSAGE	:45
TROT	1:12
WALK	:32
CANTER	2:04
TROT	:24
PASSAGE	:45
Total Ride Time	5:42

A horse performing this ride has to have great strength and gaits to start with passage, a glitter of the most difficult movement, maintain sparkle during the walk, trot and canter segments, and still be able to bedazzle the judge and audience with the ending passage.

Whichever method you decide to use, keep in mind this notion of "theme." Music, as an unspoken language, conveys attitudes, feelings, and moods. Consider the old silent movie films where a local piano player would create the suspense of a chase, the thrill of a rescue, the tenderness of a love scene, or the sadness of tragedy. This is an example of matching emotions with the actors through the use of music to take you from one mood to another. Television does the same thing today; try sitting back and concentrating on what music does for the story. You will want to approach your musical freestyle in the same way: let the music and choreography speak for you.

Choreographing the Ride

The first step in actually designing your ride is done with pencil and paper. It's interesting to see the geometrical patterns formed by drawing and creating your ride on paper. To start, here's a simple method to draw the arena on paper to have the proper proportions in a ratio to the 20-meter by 60-meter arena (which in reality is the length 3 times the width).

To prepare a scaled down form on paper:

(1) Draw 3 circles of equal diameter in a row touching each other (you can use a glass or jar lid).

(2) Enclose the circles by drawing the rectangle around them, touching the outer extremities of each circle.

(3) The placement of the letters around the edge of the arena serves only as markers to identify your ride. The compulsory movements need not be executed at the letters.

You should prepare at least a dozen sheets with the diagram of the arena.

It might be helpful to prepare a list of the compulsory movements required for the level you wish to ride; let the official score sheets be your guide.

You start to choreograph a ride by simply diagraming the movements that you can do well and like to do, according to the level at which you are working. This will be the "bank" that you draw from in designing the ride. As you do this, you will be able to see the artistic and symmetrical balance of the composition develop from these movements.

I recommend opening the ride with a movement you feel especially good about doing. If you like to do it, chances are that you do it well. By starting the ride with a strong "show-off" movement, you'll have an attention-getting opening with a well-performed technical and artistic demonstration of the ability of the horse and rider.

What you put where in the ride can work to your advantage. You must be keenly aware of your and your horse's strongest and weakest points, and design your ride taking them into account. Be conservative with the movements you have not completely mastered or, when possible, leave them out. Since you design the ride, you can show the true strengths of your horse and the key movements within the level you are presenting. Let your motto be "Don't bite off more than you can chew," by entering with a ride that is beyond your or your horse's level of ability.

Also keep in mind while you design your ride that when you perform a compulsory movement on one rein only, the judge has only one chance for the technical appraisal of that move

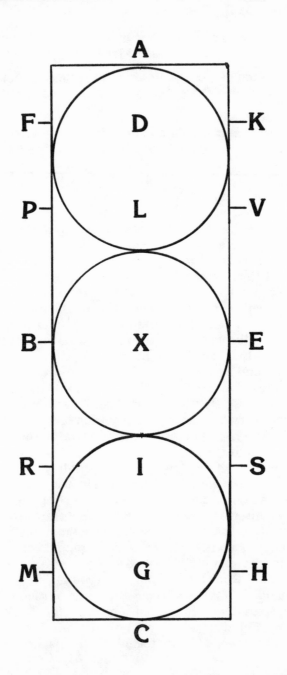

ment. You need to choose with care on which rein a particular movement will best be presented.

As you design your ride, put yourself in the judge's seat and consider what it will look like from that perspective. You should be very aware of what the judge can see from this angle of vision. This may even help you decide where to place the stronger (or weaker!) movements.

The appropriate movements must fit with the time allowed for the level being presented. You must comply with this and all of the rules applicable to your level (see the Appendix).

It is important to use the whole arena as your "stage." Do not confine your ride to one side or the center. Plan the transitions in places to give you plenty of space. For example, don't charge down the centerline and find that you are ahead of the music and have no place to go for a transition except the judge's lap!

Do things during the walk segments. It is not necessary to stay on a straight line. If it is a collected walk, why not ride a shoulder-in? Your inventiveness in combining the cleverness of composition with correctness of execution will earn you rewards. You should think of variations in the movements. A ride that resembles a compulsory test will not be considered creative or interesting.

The ending of a musical freestyle performance is a highly important affair which you as the rider/choreographer should be as concerned about as the playright is with his third act curtain.

Spend as many hours as necessary shaping and redoing the final ending. If the end of the action and music closes on a weak illogical conclusion, the first reaction from the audience (which includes the judge!) will be one of disappointment. This last impression is not only the strongest one, but tends to color the audience's opinion of the whole performance.

Think of your ride as a three-act play, with the beginning explosive, a high spot in the middle, and the ending stimulating, surprising and lasting.

Your performance can be set apart from all others if your freestyle relates to a dance feeling with a well constructed choreographic design. A symmetrical and fluent ride is beautiful because it requires an enormous degree of riding principles, with one required movement flowing smoothly and capably to another.

Take the time when riding to experiment with the combination and transitions of the movements you are planning. At the same time, come back to the drawing board and analyze the composition and performance. Remember, preparing a ride does take time. It's a matter of working between what you diagram on paper and the actual riding of the diagrams. Working with the diagrams on paper is a good starting point and will help you practice the ride away from the horse. You'll be surprised at how many riding benefits will follow the use of paper and pencil!

Timing and Editing the Ride

After you have a good general idea of your ride, you'll need to time it with horse and rider. You'll need your helper again with a stop watch or conventional watch with a second hand.

The official riding time is started after the salute and ends with the final salute. Two important reminders: movements exceeding the level of difficulty will be penalized by a deduction of four points for each that takes place, and you are permitted to use in your particular freestyle any combination of gaits or movements allowed in the declared level.

Let's assume you are going to do a five-minute ride. Do not be disappointed if during the first timing, you are over or under: that's natural! The compulsory movements have to stay in the ride no matter what, so what do you do? You have to be creative to determine what, or where you can add or subtract from the ride.

The first place to consider is the transition points between gaits; they can be shortened or extended as needed. The next option is to work with the timing within each gait. An example would be if you are running overtime and you are trotting from M–X–K. Try the change to M–E instead. Also, another possibility is to shorten the walk. These are simple ideas. Soon you will get very adept at changing sequences and working with seconds. The process at this stage is to keep changing, ride and time again, until you fit all the required movements into the five- or six-minute period. Some movements need only be shown in one direction. Be sure and check the score sheet for the required compulsory movements.

It is wise to be 5 or 10 seconds short of the time allowed because movements performed after the time allowed will not be considered by the judges, and the ride will be penalized by the deduction of two points from the total score. Further, the dressage arena footing or even a slight variance in size can alter a ride by these important seconds. The audio equipment and judge's equipment can also deviate by seconds from your equipment.

After you are satisfied with the technical composition of the ride, you have timed each segment and you are within a safe limit, it will be time for the next step in the creative process.

Adding the Music

Now here you are with a nice organized ride, all the segments correctly timed, with no music. It's time to start working with the musical selections you've been making all along.

Again, do not be disappointed if when you first try the music and ride together, they do not exactly match; it would be highly unusual if they did! What you are doing now is refining your ride, putting on the finishing touches. This will be a process of altering the transitions, with a change in gaits or within specific movements.

The factor that becomes prominent at this time is the phrasing. Remember that a phrase is a musical sentence. Changes of gait or in a movement should coincide with a musical phrase. You need to work back and forth between the ride and the phrasing to balance the two.

For example, suppose that during the first attempt for matching the music, you have timed the trot work at one minute and 51 seconds. It will be almost impossible to have in your chosen music a phrase ending at exactly one minute and 51 seconds. Use your timer with the music and find the phrase ending either before or after the one minute and 51 seconds. Phrases may vary within eight to twenty-four seconds in length. Whether you decide to use more or less music will be contingent upon adjusting the trot time and to balancing the allocated time to the other gaits. After this work is finished, you will just have to make minor adjustments in the ride to fit in with the musical phrases. This is one of the freedoms you enjoy in the musical freestyle: you do not have to end a movement at a letter. You have the whole arena to work with and *you* get to decide where things go!

There is another way to work with the ride and music. You can use your VCR to help. To do this have a videotape made of the whole ride as you had it worked within the time allotted. Edit the music as close as possible with phrase endings to match for each gait. You can save time by working indoors, and have the fun of watching your musical freestyle ride develop. Once you have reached this stage, you will only have the minor riding adjustments to make to the music.

A Special Word About Entrance Music

Entrance music for a musical freestyle ride can be very dramatic and set the stage for the solo performance. The judge looks up, the audience looks up; and it captivates one's eyes to the on-stage musical freestyle performer.

If you perform your ride without entrance music, you will miss a very joyful 20 or 30 seconds. The entrance music will do pleasant things for you. First, you the rider, will feel a stimulation that will set you in a dancing mood for the performance. Music stirs the emotions, produces a beat, rhythm and a titillation that you can revel in. In addition, the audience is called to attention and subconsciously shares this glowing feeling with you. Showmanship, the art of dressage, and music will captivate those that are in listening and viewing realm.

The entrance or "lead-in music" as it is called should be in the same mood or tone as the trot or canter music for your ride. However, if you use a fanfare music for the entrance of the ride, it is not necessary to check the tempo. Fanfare music is a dramatic musical prelude, not necessarily at an even tempo.

You have 90 seconds to get into the arena after the bell rings. This is your 90 seconds of prime time; use it gainfully. As you smile and ride around the outside perimeter of the dressage arena, all eyes are upon you. Instill in your mind a "pre-entry" check list: Hands, where are they and what are they doing? Feet and legs, are they where you know they should be? Are you sitting on *two* seat bones with nice posture of back and head? And finally, check the rhythm and tempo of the horse. Your confidence will shine through the entrance music and announce a performance is about to take place. You will sense a hush from the audience as they are preparing with you for a very pleasant performance.

Here is the quickest way to time and find your starting point outside of the dressage arena to commence with the musical freestyle fanfare or entrance music. For timing purposes, reverse the entry by riding out of the arena in this manner:

- Halt at X facing A.

- When the entrance music starts, ride out of the arena, turning right or left, whichever you prefer.

Let's assume your music ends at P.

- Take a good look at where you are. Turn around and position yourself on the same spot.

- Now ride in when the music starts. When it ends, you will be at X facing C and the judge.

What has been established is a definite point for the music to be started for the entry. The halt does not have to be at X; it could be anywhere on center line. When the judge rings the bell for your entry, you will be somewhere warming up around the arena to the right. As pre-arranged with the audio controller, as you arrive at P the music will start. At the final crescendo of music, you will find yourself at X, and halting perfectly with the music.

The entrance music does not count toward the total allotted time for the ride. The timing starts after the halt and salute, and

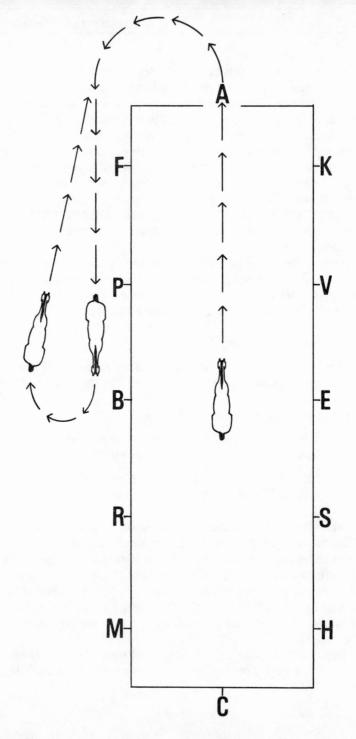

ends with the final halt and salute included. Practice this quick method of timing the entrance music several times and enjoy the perfect timing at the halt of music, horse, and rider.

Chapter 7

Preparing the Cassette Tape

There are a number of ways to have a cassette tape made for your freestyle ride. The method you use will depend on your time, equipment, and resources. Many riders are limited with time because of training and showing multiple horses. Another group may not have the basic equipment or music resources. They will then choose to have a tape made for them by a professional. In my experience, though, the majority of riders are in earnest about wanting to learn to produce their own cassette tape.

Of course you could improve the quality of your tape by using expensive, sophisticated equipment in a studio, or with the help of a musical arranger, or even a full 96-piece orchestra. But you can also produce a perfectly usable tape using the equipment readily available to most people.

If you have, or have the use of, a stereo component that plays records and cassette tapes, you can with effort and patience make a tape to use that will be of as good quality as those of world class riders.

Cassette Tapes

For best home results, start with a new, high quality, low noise, 30-minute tape, with 15 minutes on each side. Consider these key cassette tape features:

1. Compatible with virtually all cassette decks.

2. Low noise and high output.

3. Good overall sound quality and reliability.

When you purchase a cassette package it will have an audio cassette selector guide to choose from. Available are: Type I–Normal, Type II–CrO$_2$ (chrome) and Type III–Metal. There will be three or four degrees of quality available for each type. The Type I - Normal bias tape is the best quality for music recorded on any equipment or at the normal switch position. I might also add that the Type I can be played on any equipment, very important for musical freestyle tapes. Before using the tape, run the blank tape all the way forward and rewind; this will eliminate weak points or looseness.

The quality and type of tape used has a lot to do with the capabilities of your equipment, so you should use the right tape for your particular recording needs. There is the bias general purpose tape for music or voice recording that can be used on any equipment or at the normal switch position. I suggest using this bias tape because when taking a tape from show to show, you never know what audio equipment will be available.

Boom-Box

If you have no equipment and want to buy a stereo dual cassette player/recorder, the best type is known as the "boom-box." They are available in diverse sizes and prices, and there is an incredible selection on the market.

The best "boom-box" has two large speakers which should be four inches in diameter or larger, a carrying handle, a good bass (for emphasis), a pause control, and most important, can be operated on either A/C or D/C current. Additional features available are a radio, double cassettes with continuous play (tape B to tape A), the ability to play records with an auxillary source, a three-digit tape counter, capability to record cassette tapes, and dubbing capabilities (tape B to tape A). A D/C (battery operated) boom-box is very handy to use where no electrical outlet is available, and will enable you to have music for your daily riding session.

The boom-box can be awkward to handle while mounted on a horse and trying to control the cassette operation. I found a very simple way is to hang the box on a fence or tree at the height a rider can manage from the back of a horse. Simple electrical house wire (#14/2) can be purchased by the foot at any hardware store. You should purchase a total of 4 feet and use 2 feet attached to each side of the handle. The remainder can be bent and shaped around most any object that is easily accessible to you while mounted. The advantage of this electrical wire is that it is easily bent, retains its shape, and is strong enough to hold the "boom-box."

Recording Instructions for Making a Cassette Tape

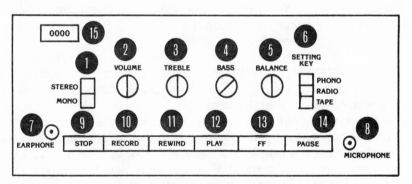

Stereo Music Control System

Set the volume at zero (#2).

Set the switch for Stereo or Mono on to "Stereo" (#1)

Set "Bass" (#4) a little stronger than medium, about three-quarters.

Set "Balance" (#5) at medium.

Function "Setting Key" (#6):
1. Set on phono if taking from a record.
2. Set on tape if using a microphone.
3. Set on radio if using a radio.
4. Use microphone (#8) jack and separate microphone when using "tape" only to make a "tape."

Depress "Record" (#10) and "Play" (#12) at the same time keeping the volume at zero (#2).

When "Counter" (#15) gets to 002, depress "Pause" (#14). This gives you a little lead tape.

Not all recording machines will have the controls as shown here. Others may have additional controls. These instructions are intended as a guide; you can adapt them for the recording machine you are going to use. A reminder, before using the tape, run the blank tape forward all the way, then rewind. After you have recorded some music on the tape, play it back to check how well you were able to follow instructions.

After what you feel is an adequate period of practice, try making a practice tape using the procedure you have learned. Select your music and arrange it in the sequence that will best suit your needs for a practice tape.

To increase your familiarity with music, make the tape with different styles of music, preferably with a strong beat. It is a kind of blending that takes place, just like baking a cake, by the accurate measurement of all the ingredients, emerges the "success baker." You will have an immediate emotional reaction when the right feeling between music, horse and rider takes place.

If you do not have a boom-box for your cassette tape, or a place to hang it for practice, invest in a portable "walk-man." Like any other piece of equipment, you will find a high and low price range. But, the first priority is to shop for a "walk-man" that will clip on to your belt and hang horizontally. Attach it as close as you can to your belt buckle, so there will be no interference from your hands. As a safety feature, you should also use the shoulder strap that will come with the walk-man. Using a walk-man gives you the freedom to ride with music without having to stay in a restricted area.

Be very vocal in your first riding session with music. If you start with a walk, count the rhythm out loud: 1 — 2 — 3 — 4, in time with the music while feeling for the same 1 — 2 — 3 — 4 movement from your horse. Work the same way at the trot (1—2) and canter (1—2—3). Remember, the tempo remains the same for each rhythm of the horse; rely on the steady beat of the music to be your guide.

The best exercise I have found for warming up the horse and rider is to ride in the trot from one change of rein across the diagonal to the other. This will test your ability to maintain the tempo, and crossing at X will make you very alert to the music and your own transition.

In addition, you will quickly know how your horse feels. He may be energetic, hurrying, or more stiff still to one side. You will even be surprised how you can detect a lameness from working with the horse from one diagonal to the other: the rhythm will be uneven.

What about the rider? Your problems will be different. How square are you sitting in the saddle? Which leg do you need to use more? Are your hands soft, too high, or are you hanging on one rein? Are the hands giving? The checklist for horse and rider problems can be extensive. By working on both sides of the horse and rider and staying in tempo, the harmony will come with the practice, and every little problem will work its way out. I like to refer to this as the balancing exercise.

The important thing is to know when *you* are correct. After all, when the music is right for the horse, it is up to you to be consistent and in control of the tempo.

Preparing the Tape for the Choreographed Ride

Now that you've become familiar with the taping process, you can begin to make the tape for your choreographed ride. This is not a one-step process, with the final version produced on the first attempt. Think of this as a preliminary tape which will be refined and polished into the final version. Here's a checklist of what you'll need to get started:

- The records or tapes you've selected with the correct beats per minute for your horse at all three gaits. These selections will come from the music you like best on the practice tape you made earlier and have been riding to.
- Your choreographed ride drawn in the diagrams.
- The segments of each gait from the choreographed ride, timed as to the length where each music or tempo change will take place.
- The entrance music, with the length timed.
- A stopwatch set to zero.
- The tape machine's counter set to zero.

You'll need to allow a bit for the tape's lead time, at least 002 or 004 on the counter.

First, record the entrance music if you are using it. When it finishes, turn the volume to zero and quickly depress "Pause." This is where the horse and rider will come to a halt in the actual ride. Allow five seconds of blank tape (record at "0" volume). The salute conducted in silence indicates that the entrance is over and the official timing of the ride will begin when the music is resumed. Change the record or tape.

Let's assume you now need two minutes and 28 seconds of trot music. You will have noted that most records or tapes have the number of minutes and seconds of play after each title. Usually this will be after the song title on the jacket and, of course, your prepared cards record this information, too. Don't forget to do your own time check of the length of play.

The secret of working with time, minutes, and seconds is to change everything into seconds. Suppose the piece of music for the trot that you want to use is three minutes and eight seconds in duration. Write it this way.

Music on record	3:08	=	188 seconds
Trot music needed	2:28	=	<u>148</u> seconds
Record time longer by			40 seconds

This is where the concept of musical *phrases* comes in and your listening technique is put into practice. Remember that a phrase is a short musical thought, at least two but typically four measures in length. The phrase is a natural division of the melody, and the time of one phrase will generally measure the same for each phrase in the whole song. If you measure 15 seconds for a phrase, and need 30 seconds of music to ride to, it will take two phrases.

For best results, it is important to stop at the end of a phrase when recording, even if you are short or over the needed time. This will prevent abruptness in the music and keep it flowing. After you have made the preliminary tape and tried it with the ride, it will be an easy matter to adjust the ride slightly to make it work.

There are two ways to eliminate the excess music of 40 seconds in our example:

1. If the trot music is being used for anything other than the very end of the ride, time the music from the beginning for two minutes and 28 seconds. Then select the nearest phrase ending either before or after. The phrase ending could make your trot music a little longer or shorter by seconds. You then just adjust the trot part of the ride.

2. If the trot music is being used as the final ending of the ride, take advantage of the music building up to

a grand finish. To do this, time 40 seconds into the music from the beginning. You may be a little early or a little late for a phrase beginning, but that's all right. Adjust your ride again and you will have another advantage of a nice ending of music for the final halt and salute.

While you are recording all the music that will play during your ride, make a note using the counter of where each segment begins. With a little practice using the "Pause" control with the counter, you'll be able to come in at the precise moment with your next musical segment.

Now you are ready to test the music tape and the ride in the arena. You can re-record, shorten, or add segments to make the uniformity that is necessary. As you ride, have your helper use the stopwatch and make notes where you need to change. The key is to be patient, the first tape is always hardest to do. You may have to go back and forth several times between the riding and recording to make a successful tape.

Using a Recording Studio

You may wish to take your tape and the timed segments of your ride to a recording studio for a more professional finish. Check the yellow pages of the telephone book for "Recording Studio." To have your tape made professionally, you actually "rent" the studio services.

Making your finished tape in a studio has another advantage because of the superior audio equipment. One of the many factors contributing to the sonic improvement of cassette recordings is the use of Dolby suppressors in nearly all better recordings and playing equipment. A Dolby is a gadget that reduces the background noises of recorded music.

Tapes made with Dolby equipment should be played on audio units made to accept them. The switch setting would be "Dolby-In." Many tapes are made on audio equipment that does not include a Dolby unit. These can be recorded with a minimum of background noise and played on audio units without the Dolby function. The studio can furnish two tapes for you, a Dolby-in and a Dolby-out.

This is important when you consider that each show you attend may have a different sound system. Be prepared: it is always safer to take the two music tapes to a competition.

Each competitor should contact the show management to arrange ahead of time with the person who will run the sound equipment to sound-check the tapes, and to submit special instructions such as when to push the "play" button at the start of the ride. The usual way for the rider to signal the sound booth is with a raise of the hand.

With the choice of tapes, you will have quality sound projection for your performance whatever the audio equipment used. Be sure that each tape is labeled on the music side with the competitor's name, horse's name, music theme, and level of the ride.

Usually an hourly rate of approximately $35 will be quoted which includes an engineer and the use of all studio equipment. Lessor charges may apply per hour for block time, such as a four-hour minimum booking. There are separate rates per hour for staff musicians, if needed, for performing, arranging, and programming. There will also be additional charges for a track master tape, cassettes and other specialized services.

If you do proper ground work at home, the job in the studio can be accomplished within four hours, depending on how many pieces of music you have to be joined. First prepare your musical freestyle program on paper with all the details about the music and time to be used. Here is a sample of a Third Level ride ready to be studio recorded:

Theme — FRENCH MUSIC

RECORD #	GAIT AND NAME OF MUSIC	TIME
605	ENTRANCE MUSIC—"Can Can"	:30
	(start at 1:50 into music until the end - 2:20)	
	HALT—SILENT TIME ON TAPE	:05
234	TROT—"Poor People of Paris"	:56
	(1st part of music)	
266	WALK—"C'est Sibone"	:47
	(start 43 seconds into music to end 1:30)	
958	CANTER—"Can Can"	1:54
	(use all of music)	
234	TROT—"Poor People of Paris"	1:14
	(start 1:00 into music to end 2:14)	
	TOTAL RIDE TIME	4:51

There are two studio recording methods. The first is reel-to-reel tape, where two large reels are used. The recording tape rolls slowly from one to the other. These reels are quite long and are "two-track" recordings, thus giving the stereo sound. The advantage of this system over recording on cassettes is that you can pinpoint sounds, one note at a time if need be, to join musical phrases.

The second method is digital recording. The electronic, digital processing of sound is now a reality. With this method, the alteration of the original musical sounds can happen in many ways: the tape being made can be spliced, the speed can be changed, phrase patterns can be repeated, and by using filters, the characteristics of sounds can be changed. This high-tech, precision recording method with its ability to change, edit and re-arrange music has grown and developed to such an extent that the sound-recording industry will probably convert to digital recording entirely in the near future.

With the high-tech equipment available at the studio, your tape will be refined by eliminating switch noises, brassy horn sounds, and so on. The musical phrase endings will have true musical note "cut-offs." The music can be faded in or out to soften, when moving from one gait and music transition to another with no loss of tempo.

This is a real asset for the rider, helping to alert him or her and prevent quick or rough transitions. The edited tape should flow smoothly, as if it were one continuous piece of music. Under the rules, a rider can be penalized for music editing that is unpleasant to the ear.

Speed Changes

Changes in the tempo of music are best left to the experts in a recording studio. The reason is that to make changes in tempo, you also change the pitch from normal to high or low which can give an undesirable audio effect.

To understand what a change in pitch would mean, consider the recordings by "The Chipmunks" popular at Christmas time, or by playing a record at the wrong speed such as a 33⅓ record played at the 78 speed. This makes the music faster but alters the pitch to a comedic point that inspires laughter to the listener. An exception to this is the high tech, expensive equipment used in recording studios. Even though you have music you like and need the tempo increased or decreased, don't consider a change greater than 12 percent. Also, the quality of music is better if the tempo needed is decreased rather than increased.

There are moderately priced "variable speed control" tape recorders available through some supply stores but as of now, they do not give acceptable performance to meet my standards. If you find a piece of music that you absolutely *must* use and it is a tempo that needs altering, by all means take it to a recording studio and have it changed with high-quality studio equipment that can balance the tone and sound. You can then decide about how the new sound will project. This is another music area for you to consider as you continue to work with the music for your musical freestyle ride.

Some Final Tips

Tapes can be erased by accident. Once you are completely satisfied with the ride and tape, *break out the safety tabs,* or non-erase clips on the tape so it cannot be accidentally erased. Each side has its own tab. This will prevent you from losing all of the time and work invested.

You should make two finished tapes, one for showing, and one to use as a practice tape which will also serve as a spare. As mentioned earlier, ideally one of these tapes is Dolby-in and the other Dolby-out. If a competition's audio equipment is compatible with Dolby-in, use it; if not, you are still prepared with Dolby-out. Your practice tape will be the Dolby-out and used in your portable boom-box.

I highly stress the necessity of replacing the batteries prior to making a tape or using the "boom-box" for a show when no electricity is available. Equipment failures are frustrating!

This book has presented the basis on which a musical freestyle ride can be developed to the highest degree.

I hope you are inspired. One of the greatest delights in riding is the special communication between a rider, his horse and music. May you continue "Dancing With Your Horse."

Appendix 1
Official Score Sheets

TECHNICAL EXECUTION

TIME LIMIT:
5 minutes

FIRST LEVEL

COMPULSORY MOVEMENTS	POSSIBLE POINTS	PRELIMINARY MARKS	CO-EFFICIENT	JUDGE'S FINAL MARKS	REMARKS
1. Walk (minimum 20 meters)	10				
2. 10-meter circle in trot	10				
3. Leg-yield in trot	10				
4. Lengthen stride in trot	10				
5. 10-meter circle in canter	10				
6. Change of lead through trot	10				
7. Lengthen stride in canter	10				
8. Freedom and regularity of gaits	10				
9. Impulsion	10				
10. Submission	10				
11. General impression of overall technical quality (including suitability of difficulty, transitions, execution of non-required movements and figures)	10		2		

TOTAL FOR TECHNICAL EXECUTION

Further Remarks:

ARTISTIC IMPRESSION

NO.

	POSSIBLE POINTS	JUDGE'S MARKS	CO-EFFICIENT	FINAL MARKS	REMARKS
MUSICALITY					
1. Appropriateness of music to horse/rider combination	10				
2. Suitability of music to rhythms and tempos of horse's gaits	10		2		
3. Cohesiveness of music: a. Composition b. Editing and recording quality	10				
CHOREOGRAPHY					
4. Design: a. Balance (left/right, gaits, paces); b. Use of space; c. Continuity of composition	10				
5. Creativity (non test-like)	10		2		
PRESENTATION					
6. Interpretation (of music, choreography & phrasing)	10		2		
7. Impact	10		2		
8. Harmony between horse and rider, (dancing quality, ease of movements)	10				

TOTAL FOR ARTISTIC IMPRESSION	120	**ARTISTIC IMPRESSION**	
TOTAL FOR TECHNICAL EXECUTION	120	**TECHNICAL EXECUTION**	
POSSIBLE POINTS	240	**TOTAL POINTS**	(See USDF Freestyle Rules on back)
		DEDUCTIONS	
Further Remarks:		**FINAL SCORE**	
		PERCENTAGE	

TECHNICAL EXECUTION

TIME LIMIT: 5 minutes

SECOND LEVEL

COMPULSORY MOVEMENTS	POSSIBLE POINTS	PRELIMINARY MARKS	CO-EFFICIENT	JUDGE'S FINAL MARKS	REMARKS
1. Walk minimum 20 meters (including turn on haunches, if shown)	10				
2. Shoulder-in at trot	10				
3. Travers in trot	10				
4. Medium trot	10				
5. 10-meter circle in canter	10				
6. Simple change of lead	10				
7. Medium canter	10				
8. Freedom and regularity of gaits	10				
9. Impulsion	10				
10. Submission	10				
11. General impression of overall technical quality (including suitability of difficulty, transitions, execution of non-required movements and figures)	10		2		

TOTAL FOR TECHNICAL EXECUTION

Further Remarks:

ARTISTIC IMPRESSION

NO.

	POSSIBLE POINTS	JUDGE'S MARKS	CO-EFFICIENT	FINAL MARKS	REMARKS
MUSICALITY					
1. Appropriateness of music to horse/rider combination	10				
2. Suitability of music to rhythms and tempos of horse's gaits	10		2		
3. Cohesiveness of music: a. Composition b. Editing and recording quality	10				
CHOREOGRAPHY					
4. Design: a. Balance (left/right, gaits, paces); b. Use of space; c. Continuity of composition	10				
5. Creativity (non test-like)	10		2		
PRESENTATION					
6. Interpretation (of music, choreography & phrasing)	10		2		
7. Impact	10		2		
8. Harmony between horse and rider, (dancing quality, ease of movements)	10				

TOTAL FOR ARTISTIC IMPRESSION	120	**ARTISTIC IMPRESSION**	
TOTAL FOR TECHNICAL EXECUTION	120	**TECHNICAL EXECUTION**	
POSSIBLE POINTS	240	**TOTAL POINTS**	
		DEDUCTIONS	
Further Remarks:		**FINAL SCORE**	
		PERCENTAGE	

(See USDF Freestyle Rules on back)

TECHNICAL EXECUTION

TIME LIMIT:
5 minutes

THIRD LEVEL

COMPULSORY MOVEMENTS	POSSIBLE POINTS	PRELIMINARY MARKS	CO-EFFICIENT	JUDGE'S FINAL MARKS	REMARKS
1. Walk minimum 20 meters (including pirouettes, if shown)	10				
2. Half-pass in collected trot	10				
3. Extended trot	10				
4. Half-pass in collected canter	10				
5. Counter canter	10				
6. Flying change of lead	10				
7. Extended Canter	10				
8. Freedom and regularity of gaits	10				
9. Impulsion	10				
10. Submission	10				
11. General impression of overall technical quality (including suitability of difficulty, transitions, execution of non-required movements and figures)	10		2		

TOTAL FOR TECHNICAL EXECUTION

Further Remarks:

ARTISTIC IMPRESSION

NO.

	POSSIBLE POINTS	JUDGE'S MARKS	CO-EFFICIENT	FINAL MARKS	REMARKS
MUSICALITY					
1. Appropriateness of music to horse/rider combination	10				
2. Suitability of music to rhythms and tempos of horse's gaits	10		2		
3. Cohesiveness of music: a. Composition b. Editing and recording quality	10				
CHOREOGRAPHY					
4. Design: a. Balance (left/right, gaits, paces); b. Use of space; c. Continuity of composition	10				
5. Creativity (non test-like)	10		2		
PRESENTATION					
6. Interpretation (of music, choreography & phrasing)	10		2		
7. Impact	10		2		
8. Harmony between horse and rider, (dancing quality, ease of movements)	10				

TOTAL FOR ARTISTIC IMPRESSION	120	**ARTISTIC IMPRESSION**	
TOTAL FOR TECHNICAL EXECUTION	120	**TECHNICAL EXECUTION**	
POSSIBLE POINTS	240	**TOTAL POINTS**	
		DEDUCTIONS	
Further Remarks:		**FINAL SCORE**	
		PERCENTAGE	

(See USDF Freestyle Rules on back)

USDF FREESTYLE RULES

1. Time limit: 5 minutes. Movements performed after the time allowed will not be scored. Two (2) points will be deducted from the total points for exceeding the time limit. There is no minimum time requirement. The ride is timed and judged from the horse's move off after the initial halt and salute. Timing will cease at the final halt. Judging will cease at the final salute.

2. Music is mandatory.

3. The rider does not submit a written copy of the choreography pattern to the judges or management.

4. Rider may carry a whip in freestyle classes. In the case of local or regional championships, management may opt to follow AHSA championship rules, which do not allow whips in championship classes. In such cases, check the prize list.

5. Only conventional attire and turnout is appropriate for riding in freestyle classes. [See AHSA Rule Book]

6. Compulsory movements may be performed in any order. Exhibitors are not required to include each movement on both reins. However, each horse should display suppleness and fluidity in both directions.

7. If a compulsory movement is not shown, a score of "0" will be given.

8. Movements exceeding the level of difficulty will be penalized by a deduction of four (4) points for each occurrence from the total points.
   a. Movements are: leg-yield, rein-back, shoulder-in, travers, renvers, half-pass at trot and canter, flying change, pirouette, turn on the haunches, piaffe and passage.
   b. Any combinations or transitions composed of elements (gaits or movements) permitted in the declared level, are permitted in the Freestyle, even if the resulting specific transition or combination is found in higher level tests.
   EXCEPTION: Tempi flying changes at Third Level are not permitted. Tempi changes are those recurring in regular sequence (of 4 strides or less).
   c. There are no limitations on size, shape or combination of figures, even if the resulting configuration is found in higher level tests.
   d. The above considerations should be given the broadest possible interpretation for the benefit of the competitor.

9. Those movements not listed on the score sheets and that do not exceed the difficulty of the level can be rewarded or penalized under "General Impression of Overall Technical Quality" on the Technical side of the score sheet.

10. Two sets of marks, one for technical execution and one for artistic impression, are given by the judge. Each set of marks is totaled separately, then added together and converted to the final percentage (%) score.

11. At the USDF levels (First, Second and Third Levels), any point spread is allowed between the Technical and Artistic scores.

12. In case of a tie, the higher total for artistic impression will break the tie. [Please note that for the AHSA/FEI freestyles (Fourth, Intermediate I and Grand Prix) ties are broken by the higher technical score. 1988-89 *AHSA Rule Book*, page 165.]

13. If the music source fails, the competitor may (time permitting and at the discretion of management): 1. restart immediately; or 2. be rescheduled to perform the freestyle in its entirety at some later time during the competition.

14. Both the technical and artistic portions of USDF freestyles at USDF/AHSA recognized competitions must be judged by AHSA licensed dressage judges. AHSA officials may judge the following levels:
   AHSA 'I' — Training Level through Grand Prix
   AHSA 'R' — Training Level through Fourth Level
   AHSA 'r' — Training Level through Second Level

15. Current USDF Freestyle Score Sheets (First, Second and Third Levels) must be used at USDF recognized competitions.

16. The arena shall be 20 meters x 60 meters.

17. Half-points (0.5) are allowed in scoring.

NOTES

AMERICAN HORSE SHOWS ASSOCIATION, INC. ™

The object of the AHSA Freestyle Test has many aspects, including the following:

For the competitor it provides an opportunity to be creative, to work with musical accompaniment, to emphasize the horse's strong points and permits an evaluation of the performance in terms of creativity and artistic content in addition to the usual technical criteria.

For the spectator it provides an attractive approach to dressage by placing it in a musical setting, thus enhancing its artistic appeal.

AHSA Freestyle Test
FOURTH LEVEL

COMPETITOR'S NAME: _____

HORSE: _____   Maximum Time: 6 Minutes

TECHNICAL EXECUTION

COMPULSORY MOVEMENTS (MAY BE PERFORMED IN ANY SEQUENCE)	POSSIBLE POINTS	PRELIMINARY MARKS	JUDGE'S MARKS	CO-EFFICIENT	TOTAL	REMARKS
1. COLLECTED WALK, INCL. HALF-PIROUETTES (20-30m)	10					
2. EXTENDED WALK (20-30 m)	10					
3. COLLECTED TROT, INCL. HALF-PASS RIGHT AND LEFT	10					
4. EXTENDED TROT	10					
5. COLLECTED CANTER, INCL. HALF-PASS RIGHT AND LEFT AND SINGLE FLYING CHANGES RIGHT AND LEFT	10					
6. EXTENDED CANTER	10					
7. CHANGES OF LEG, EVERY FOURTH STRIDE	10					
8. CHANGES OF LEG, EVERY THIRD STRIDE	10					
9. HALF-PIROUETTE TO THE RIGHT AT COLLECTED CANTER	10			2		
10. HALF-PIROUETTE TO THE LEFT AT COLLECTED CANTER	10			2		
11. FREEDOM & REGULARITY OF THE PACES, IMPULSION	10			2		
TOTAL FOR TECHNICAL EXECUTION	140					

NO.

ARTISTIC IMPRESSION

	POSSIBLE POINTS	JUDGE'S MARKS	CO-EFFICIENT	TOTAL	REMARKS
1. **ARTISTIC IMPRESSION** SHOWMANSHIP OF HORSE AND RIDER AS A TEAM EXPRESSION BRILLIANCE	10		4		
2. **MUSICALITY** SUITABILITY OF MUSIC TO GAITS AND MOVEMENTS APPROPRIATENESS OF MUSICAL SELECTIONS TO THE HORSE/ RIDER TEAM FLOW AND EDITING OF SELECTIONS	10		3		
3. **CHOREOGRAPHY/COMPOSITION** OVERALL USE OF ARENA VARIETY OF MOVEMENTS AND SEQUENCES RELATIONSHIP OF MOVEMENTS TO MUSIC ORIGINALITY	10		3		
TOTAL FOR ARTISTIC IMPRESSION	100				

DEDUCTIONS	
TECHNICAL EXECUTION	
TOTAL POINTS	
FINAL SCORE	
PERCENTAGE	

Time Penalty: more than 6 mins., deduct 2 points from the total for artistic impression.

The breaking of a tie will be decided by the higher marks for technical execution.

Reproduced by the kind permission of the American Horse Shows Association, Inc. © AHSA, Inc.

AHSA Freestyle Test
INTERMEDIATE 1

COMPETITOR'S NAME: _____

HORSE: _____   Maximum Time: 6 Minutes

TECHNICAL EXECUTION

COMPULSORY MOVEMENTS (MAY BE PERFORMED IN ANY SEQUENCE)	POSSIBLE POINTS	PRELIMINARY MARKS	JUDGE'S MARKS	CO-EFFICIENT	TOTAL	REMARKS
1. COLLECTED WALK, (20-30 m)	10					
2. EXTENDED WALK (20-30 m)	10					
3. COLLECTED TROT, INCL. HALF-PASS RIGHT AND LEFT	10					
4. EXTENDED TROT	10					
5. COLLECTED CANTER, INCL. HALF-PASS RIGHT AND LEFT SHOWING COUNTER-CHANGES OF HAND	10					
6. EXTENDED CANTER	10					
7. CHANGES OF LEG, EVERY THIRD STRIDE	10					
8. CHANGES OF LEG, EVERY SECOND STRIDE	10					
9. PIROUETTE TO THE RIGHT AT COLLECTED CANTER	10			2		
10. PIROUETTE TO THE LEFT AT COLLECTED CANTER	10			2		
11. FREEDOM & REGULARITY OF THE PACES, IMPULSION	10			2		
TOTAL FOR TECHNICAL EXECUTION	140					

NO.

ARTISTIC IMPRESSION

	POSSIBLE POINTS	JUDGE'S MARKS	CO-EFFICIENT	TOTAL	REMARKS
1. **ARTISTIC IMPRESSION** SHOWMANSHIP OF HORSE AND RIDER AS A TEAM EXPRESSION BRILLIANCE	10		4		
2. **MUSICALITY** SUITABILITY OF MUSIC TO GAITS AND MOVEMENTS APPROPRIATENESS OF MUSICAL SELECTIONS TO THE HORSE/ RIDER TEAM FLOW AND EDITING OF SELECTIONS	10		3		
3. **CHOREOGRAPHY/COMPOSITION** OVERALL USE OF ARENA VARIETY OF MOVEMENTS AND SEQUENCES RELATIONSHIP OF MOVEMENTS TO MUSIC ORIGINALITY	10		3		
TOTAL FOR ARTISTIC IMPRESSION	100				
			DEDUCTIONS		
			TECHNICAL EXECUTION		
			TOTAL POINTS		
			FINAL SCORE		
			PERCENTAGE		

Time Penalty: more than 6 mins., deduct 2 points from the total for artistic impression.

The breaking of a tie will be decided by the higher marks for artistic impression.

AHSA Freestyle Test
GRAND PRIX

COMPETITOR'S NAME: _____

HORSE: _____

Maximum Time: 6 Minutes
Minimum Time: 5½ Minutes

TECHNICAL EXECUTION

COMPULSORY MOVEMENTS	POSSIBLE POINTS	PRELIMINARY MARKS	JUDGE'S MARKS	CO-EFFICIENT	TOTAL	REMARKS
1. WALK (COLLECTED AND/OR EXTENDED MINIMUM 20 M)	10					
2. COLLECTED TROT INCL. HALF-PASS RIGHT AND LEFT	10					
3. EXTENDED TROT	10					
4. COLLECTED CANTER INCL. HALF-PASS RIGHT AND LEFT	10					
5. EXTENDED CANTER	10					
6. FLYING CHANGES EVERY SECOND STRIDE (MINIMUM 5 CONSECUTIVE STRIDES)	10					
7. FLYING CHANGES EVERY STRIDE (MINIMUM 5 CONSECUTIVE STRIDES)	10					
8. PIROUETTE IN CANTER RIGHT	10			2		
9. PIROUETTE IN CANTER LEFT	10			2		
10. PASSAGE (MINIMUM 20 M)	10			2		
11. PIAFFE (MINIMUM 10 STEPS)	10			2		
12. TRANSITIONS FROM PASSAGE TO PIAFFE AND VICE VERSA	10					
TOTAL FOR TECHNICAL EXECUTION	100					

NO.

ARTISTIC IMPRESSION

GENERAL IMPRESSION	POSSIBLE POINTS	JUDGE'S MARKS	CO-EFFICIENT	TOTAL	REMARKS
13. HARMONY BETWEEN RIDER AND HORSE EASE OF THE MOVEMENTS	10		6		
14* COMPOSITION OF THE PROGRAM CHOREOGRAPHY DEGREE OF DIFFICULTY AND INCORPORATION OF MUSIC	10		10		
TOTAL FOR ARTISTIC IMPRESSION	100				
		DEDUCTIONS			
		TECHNICAL EXECUTION			
		TOTAL POINTS			
		FINAL SCORE			
		PERCENTAGE			

*Mark in decimals for No. 14 only.

Time Penalty: more than 6 mins. or less that 5 mins. 30 secs., deduct 2 points from the total for artistic impression.

The breaking of a tie will be decided by the higher marks for technical execution.

Reproduced by the kind permission of the American Horse Shows Association, Inc. © AHSA, Inc.

Appendix 2
Diagrams of Musical Freestyle Rides

The diagrams of rides are examples for you to trace around and get the feeling of riding on paper. As I had mentioned, the dressage letters don't count during a freestyle ride, but they do need to be used for guidance. Preparing a ride does take time, but can be simplified by working out the basic plan. The plan that you draw on paper will provide you with a picture to project in so why not draw your presentation on paper and be the first judge to evaluate?

The choreography of a musical freestyle ride, as you already know, is an essential section of the whole plan. To diagram a ride will first get your creative juices flowing. After all of those hours of riding and perfecting the artistic and technical portion, your picture will show the balanced mixture of basic movements, and the total utilization of the arena which is your canvas. Take notice of the free flowing patterns of the diagrams. A good way to start a ride is by showing the bending and flexibility of the horse. Try for symmetrical balance, and the utilization of the whole arena. I know you will be intrigued and have fun with diagramming a ride.

First Level
Musical Freestyle Ride
Choreography by Mary E. Campbell

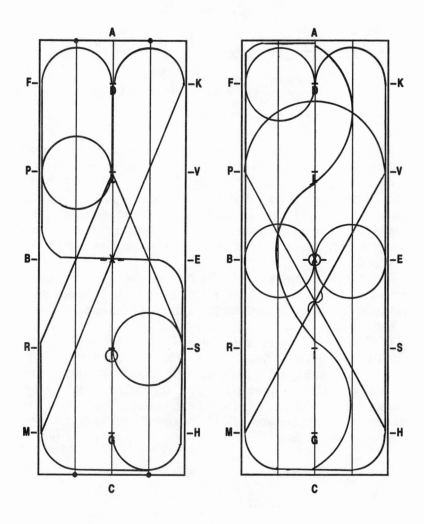

A	Enter working trot sitting
I	Halt. Salute. Proceed working trot sitting
C	Track left
S	10 meter circle left
E	Turn left
B	Turn right
P	10 meter circle right
A	Down center line
L-S	Leg yield left
M-X-K	Lengthen stride in trot sitting
A	Down center line
L-R	Leg yield right
M	Working walk
C-A	3 Loops of serpentine, on quarter lines, length of arena
A	Free walk on long rein
F-D	Half 10 meter circle left
D-K	Half 10 meter circle right
K	Working walk
V	Working canter
E	Circle right 10 meter circle

M-V	Change rein. Change of lead thru trot
V	Half 20 meter circle
B	Circle left 10 meter circle
H-P	Lengthen stride in canter
F	Working trot
A	Down center line
X	Halt. Salute

Second Level
Musical Freestyle Ride
Choreography by Mary E. Campbell

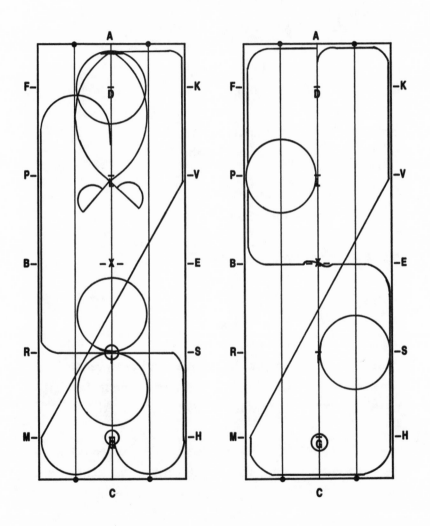

A	Enter collected trot
I	Halt. Salute. Proceed collected trot
C	Track left
S	Turn left
I	Circle right 10 meter
I	Circle left 10 meter
R	Turn right
Between P—F	Half circle right
L—X	Shoulder-in right
X—G	Traverse right
C	Turn right
M—V	Medium trot
V	Collected trot
A	Halt. Rein back 4 steps
A	Proceed medium walk
A—L	Loop right on quarter line to centerline
Between L—E	On diagonal half turn on haunches left
L—A	Loop left on quarter line to A
A—L	Loop left on quarter line to centerline
Between L—B	On diagonal half turn on haunches right
L—A	Loop right on quarter line to A

A	Medium walk. 10 meter circle
A—P	Collected canter
P	Circle left 10 meter
B	Turn left
X	Simple change of lead
E	Turn right
S	Circle right 10 meter
M—V	Medium canter
K	Collected trot
A	Down centerline
G	Halt. Salute.

Third Level
Musical Freestyle Ride

Choreography by Mary E. Campbell

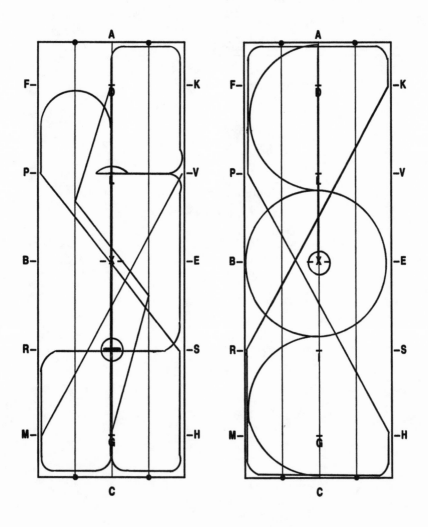

A	Enter collected canter
I	Halt. Salute. Proceed collected trot
C	Track left
S—P	Medium trot
Between P—F	Collected trot half 10 meter circle right. On centerline shoulder-in right, traverse left
C	Track right
M—V	Extended trot
K	Collected trot
A	Down centerline
Between D—G	Three counter-changes of hand in half pass. The first half pass to the right of centerline 5 meters, second to the left 5 meters, third to the right ending on centerline before G
C	Track right
M	Collected walk
R	Turn right
I	Halt. Rein back 4 steps. Proceed extended walk

S	Turn left
V	Turn left
L	Half pirouette right
V	Turn left
K	Collected canter
A	Half 20 meter circle left. No change of lead, proceed to one and a half times 20 meter circle in counter canter, proceed half 20 meter circle left to C
H—P	Extended canter
F	Collected canter
K—R	Half pass right
Between R—M	Flying change of lead
H—P	Half pass left
Between P—F	Flying change of lead
A	Down centerline
L	Collected trot
X	Halt. Salute.

Fourth Level
Musical Freestyle Ride
Choreography by Nancy S. Harris

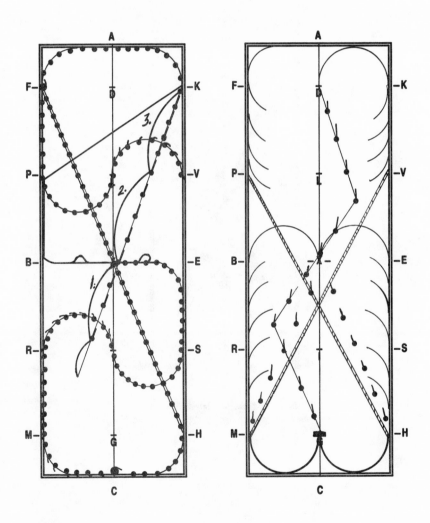

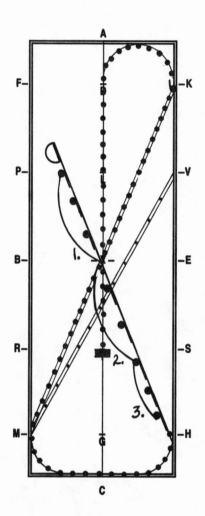

A	Enter collected trot
G	Halt. Salute, proceed collected trot
C	Track right
M—B	Shoulder-in right
B	Half circle right 10 meters, returning to M at half pass right
H—E	Shoulder-in left
E	Half circle left 10 meters, returning to H at half pass left
M—V	Medium trot
V—K	Travers left
A	Down centerline
D—G	2 counter-changes of hand in half pass to either side of centerline, the first half pass to the left and the last to the left of 5 meters, and the other to the right of 10 meters
C	Track left
H—P	Extended trot
P	Travers right
F	Collected Trot
AKPB	Extended walk
B	Collected walk and turn to E

Between X—E	Half pirouette left
Between X—B	Half pirouette right
XES	Collected canter, right lead
SI	Half circle of 10 meters right, followed by half circle left
IR	In counter canter
RMC	Counter canter
C	Flying change of leg
HXF	Extended canter
F	Collected canter and flying change of leg
K—R	Half pass right to 5 meters (quarter line), other side of centerline on quarter line half pirouette right
	Towards K, 3 flying changes of lead every 4th stride
AFP	Collected canter left lead
PL	Half circle of 10 meters left, followed by half circle right in counter canter
VM	Change rein, medium canter with no change of lead

H—I	Half pass left to 5 meters (quarter line), other side of centerline on quarter line half pirouette left
	Towards H 3 flying changes of lead every 3rd stride
MXK	Extended canter
K	Collected canter and flying change
A	Down centerline
L	Collected trot
X	Halt. Salute.

Intermediate 1
Musical Freestyle Ride
Choreography by Bent Jenson

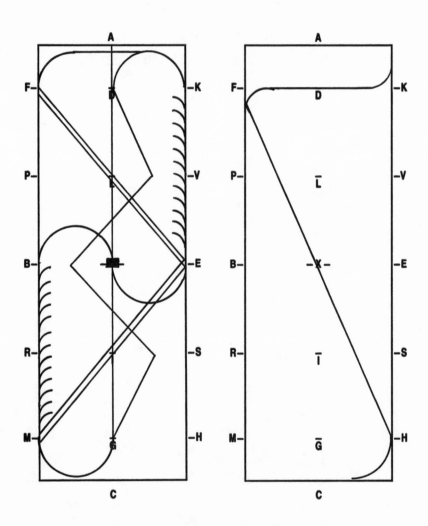

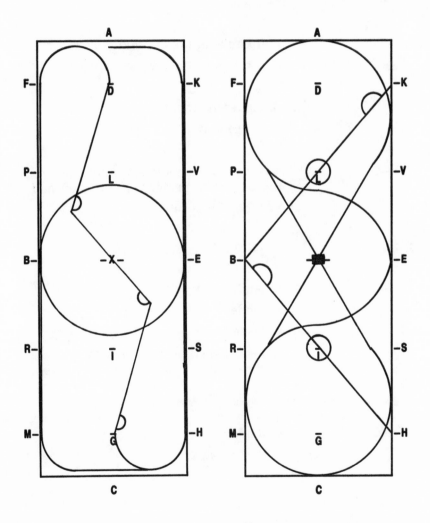

A	Enter collected canter
X	Halt. Salute. Proceed in collected trot
C	Track to the right
M—B	Shoulder-in (or travers)
B—X	Half circle 10 meters right followed by
X—E	Half circle 10 meters left
E—K	Shoulder-in (or travers)
A	Down centerline
D—G	4 half passes 5 meters to either side of the centerline beginning to the left and ending to the right
C	Track right
M—I—E	Extended trot
E—L—F	Extended trot
F	Collected Trot
K	Collected walk (or when the music changes) turn right
F	Turn left
F—X—H	Extended walk
H	Collected walk

C	Canter right lead (or when canter music starts)
R—B—E—B—P	Extended canter with 20 meter circle
P	Collected canter
A	Down centerline
D—G	3 counter changes half pass to either side of the centerline with change of leg at each change of direction, the first half pass to the right and the last to the left
C	Track left
S—E—B—E—V	Extended canter with 20 meter circle
V	Collected canter
A—C	Serpentine of 3 loops with flying changes every third stride
H—I—B	
I	Pirouette to the left
B	Flying change of leg
B—L—K	
L	Pirouette to the right
K	Flying change of leg
A—A	Figure eight. Whole arena with flying changes every second stride

A   Down centerline

X   Or halt with ending of music. Salute.

Grand Prix
Musical Freestyle Ride

Choreography by Bent Jensen

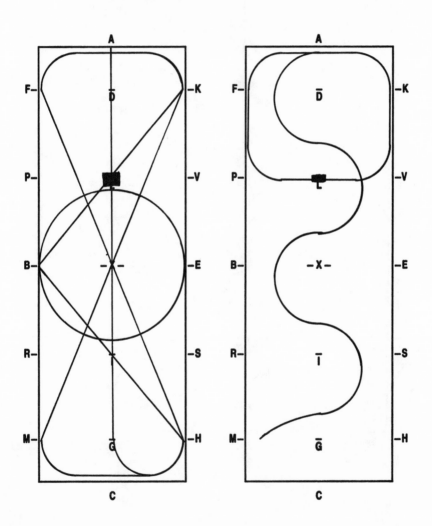

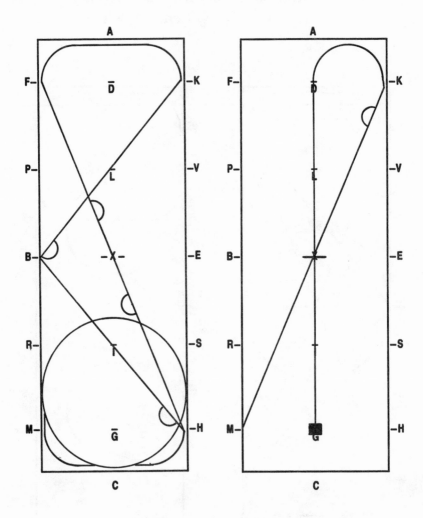

A	Enter in collected canter
L	Halt, immobility, salute, proceed in collected trot to the music
C	Track to the left
H—I—B	Half pass to the left
B—E—B	Circle 20 meters at medium trot
B—L—K	Half pass to the right
F—X—M	Extended trot
H—X—K	Extended trot
A	Passage
P	Turn left
L	Piaffe
V	Turn left
K	Collected walk
A	Serpentine of 4 loops from quarter line to quarter line with the last loop to the right
M	Left lead canter collected
C	Circle 20 meters with changes of leg every 2nd stride
H—X—F	Across the diagonal with pirouette left, one tempi changes, pirouette right
K—L—B	Half pass right in canter
B	Flying change of lead

B—I—H	Half pass left in canter
H	Flying change of lead
M—X—K	Extended canter
K	Collected canter
K	Flying change of lead
A	Turn left on the centerline
	Transitions to piaffe or passage with music
X	Piaffe
G	Halt. Salute.

Index

Bar lines, 26
Beat, 23-26. *See also*
   downbeat
Beats per minute,
   counting horse's, 36-41
   determining, 33-42
Boom box, 72-73

Canter, 18
   AHSA definition of,
      39-40
   average beats per minute
      of, 36
   rhythm, 31
   timing beats per minute,
      39-40
Cassette tapes,
   key features, 71-72
   practice tapes, 54-55
   preparing, 71-82
   preparing for
      choreographed ride,
      76-78
   recording instructions,
      73-74
   safety tabs, 82
Choreographing the ride,
   60-64

Downbeat, 23-26. *See also*
   beat
   determining tempo, 33
   origins of, 23-24
Dolby equipment, 78-79

Entrance music, 66-69

Equipment,
   boom box, 72, 73
   cassette player. *See*
      boom box
   cassette tapes, 71-72,
      73-74, 82
   Dolby, 78-79
   kitchen timer, 35
   metronome, 34-35
   stopwatch, 35-56, 42
   video cassette recorder,
      37, 66
   walk-man, 74-75

Gaits, 17-18

Impulsion, 56

Kitchen timer, 35
Kür,
   derivation of word, 14

Lungeing to music, 55-56

Measure, 26
Metronome, 34-35, 42
  use in selecting music,
    42
Music,
  American modern, 46
  changing the tempo of,
    81
  classical, 47
  double time, 47-48
  entrance, 66-69
  fanfare, 48
  folk, 44-45
  German, 41
  half-time, 47
  Latin, 45
  listening to, 51-52
  lungeing to, 55-56
  novelty, 47
  ragtime, 45
  selection of, three con-
    siderations, 48
  selecting, 43
  sources, 50
  styles of, 43-49
  suitability of to horse
    and rider, 49-50
  timing, 41
  vocal, 48
Music library,
  building a, 52-54
Music library card, 52-54
Musical freestyle ride,
  adding the music to,
    65-66

AHSA definition of, 13
basic principles, 17-21
choreographing, 60-64
ending, importance of,
  63
horse's response to, 16
lower levels, need for, 15
requirements of, 14
timing and editing,
  64-65, 77-78
value of 11-12, 13, 15

Note values, 27-29

Passage, 36, 40, 59
  average beats per minute
    of, 36
  timing beats per minute,
    40
Phrases, musical, 31-32, 65,
  77
  in editing the ride, 77
Piaffe,
  timing beats per minute,
    40

Rhythm, 18-20
  AHSA definition of, 18
Recording studio,
  methods, 80-81
  using a, 78-81

Score sheets,
  available from, 14
Show management,
  contacting prior to show,
    79

Stopwatch, 35-36, 42

Tempo, 20-21, 33, 37
   AHSA definition of, 20
   horse's inconsistency in,
      37
Theme, choosing a, 58
Time signatures, 29-31
Timers, 34-36
   kitchen timer, 35
   metronome, 34-35
   stopwatch, 35-36
Timing,
   horse's gaits, 33-40
   music, 41-42
Trot, 17-18
   AHSA definition of, 38
   average beats per minute
      of, 36

rhythm, 30
timing beats per minute,
   38

Video cassette recorder,
   use in final editing, 66
   using to determine beats
      per minute, 37

Walk, 17, 47
   AHSA definition of, 39
   average beats per
      minute, 36
   lungeing for improve-
      ment in, 56
   rhythm, 31
   timing beats per minute,
      39
Walk-man, 74-75